Ashes to Flames

Spiritual Burnout and Recovery

Kim & Kathy Wenzel

ISBN 0-7414-3571-3

Published by:

INFINITY
PUBLISHING.COM

1094 New DeHaven Street, Suite 100
West Conshohocken, PA 19428-2713
Info@buybooksontheweb.com
www.buybooksontheweb.com
Toll-free (877) BUY BOOK
Local Phone (610) 941-9999
Fax (610) 941-9959

Printed in the United States of America

Printed on Recycled Paper

Published October 2006

This Book
Ashes to Flames
is
Dedicated to Sandee Hawk

Sandee is a true Samaritan who cares and helps
wounded and hurting believers on the side of the road of life.
May God bless her for making this book possible.

Ashes to Flames

Pastor Kim & Kathy Wenzel

Spiritual Burnout and Recovery

country of Rhodesia. I was young and totally inexperienced. The haunting eyes of the dying woman have stayed with me all these years. After pastoring in a legalistic denomination for over twenty years in Canada, we moved to Colorado Springs, and met many former pastors. It was in Colorado God spoke to us and revealed our deeper calling to help the wounded of the church. Thirty years before I had no training, skill or experience with helping the wounded on the side of the road. Now with decades of experience in the church, God wants us to pick up the wounded along the road, pastor and lay-member alike, and teach them about life in the tree of life.

Here is a classic introduction to burnout. Elijah and his unrealistic expectations after the Mount Carmel shootout are explored in detail. Elijah is deeply discouraged over the fact nothing seems to have changed after the prophets of Baal are defeated. No great revival has broken out. In the end, Elijah learns first hand that big power displays don't reach inside and change people's hearts. After the wind, lightening, earthquakes and fire storms he sees from the mouth of his cave, Elijah has the same memorized answer for God as to why he is here at the cave. It dawns on Elijah that it is the still small voice that reaches inside him and renews him. It is the flow of God's very Spirit touching his spirit that creates enough healing for Elijah that he returns to his ministry – much wiser with more realistic expectations for himself, and the people of Israel.

PART THREE – HOW JESUS TAUGHT THE TREE OF LIFE APPROACH

Chapter 1

Burnout! Is that a Church Problem?

Since my birth in 1952, church attendance in North America has been in constant decline. My birth has no connection to this, but what does? Could it be the scientific method of thinking? How about the fallout of two world wars on the psyche of the human race? Perhaps we can blame it on the increase in wealth and materialism in the western world?

No doubt all these factors can be entered into the equation. But, here's one more. What about old fashioned disillusionment? Can the fact that a self-centered gospel is preached in many churches, and when all these wonderful promises never come to pass in the here and now, some become disheartened and even angry?

No doubt, many factors could be listed, many good arguments stated to support each. The bottom line is, people are streaming out of our churches. The World Christian Encyclopedia states as many as sixteen million people leave the body of Christ each year worldwide. I'm not sure how the World Christian Encyclopedia arrives at that statistic, but it is a shocker.

On the leadership side of the equation, the stats for pastoral burnout are staggering. Surveys by groups like Focus on the Family and The Pastor's Institute estimate anywhere from one thousand to fifteen hundred pastors and other ministry leaders leave their posts each month (in North America alone), many never return. Some depart for reasons of stress or illness, other leaders are fired for just and unjust causes. The Army of God is losing its officers at a tremendous rate, yet so many church members close their eyes to the problem.

To openly discuss this crisis is to admit something is failing in modern Christianity. We don't like that idea. Many believers answered their call of God because they had bottomed out at living life on their terms, and were now willing to listen to a loving God. Now, to suggest some major tenets of cultural Christianity are misleading us and setting us up for huge disappointment is to challenge the whole concept of Christianity. In reality it isn't, but some fear this is the case.

For example, Paul was very willing to discuss issues in spoken and written form. He wrote some staunch words regarding the gospel message. To Paul the gospel was God's *good news unto eternal life*. It led to life, real life. If it led anywhere else, it was a false gospel. No matter how attractive the message was, or what it promised, or how logical it sounded, if it led to disillusionment, legalism, exhaustion, or wounding, ***it was a false gospel.*** Case closed!

What gospels do we have today in North America? They are too numerous to list, but here is a sample. The health and wealth gospel, the prosperity gospel, the feel good gospel, the here's what God can do for me gospel, the bless me gospel, the prophetic gospel, the name it and claim it gospel, the faith gospel, the KJV only gospel, the easy grace gospel, the prayer of Jabez gospel, the old-time hymns only gospel, the loud contemporary worship gospel. You get the idea!

What is happening inside the organization Jesus founded on the basis of unconditional blood covenant love? What is happening inside the spiritual community that should be known for how wonderful people treat one another? What is happening inside the church that should be fueled and empowered through the Holy Spirit? What is happening to those who live by the new way of the spirit? Human politics and blunt carnality seem to rule the day inside many churches. The secular society requires a board made of people to make sure the church is run properly. That human element in that same safety system is the cause of many a church split and endless heartache.

The endless list of church growth books the pastor reads creates problems and unfulfilled expectations, followed by disillusionment. Next, the endless list of self-help books with a Biblical twist keep the pastors and members caught up in the illusion *they are in control*.

We love control. We want to worship God with all our being, yet, hang onto some element of control. It gives us the feeling we have a part to play, even if Jesus is the *author and finisher* of our faith. Even though we died in the waters of baptism, we still like the idea we can shape our life the way we want it, and God will help us do so. We call it being blessed. God calls it our attempts to manipulate him.

Pastors hurt their congregations. Boards hurt their pastors. Elders hurt deacons. Members hurt pastors. Pastors hurt pastors. Members hurt members. Where does it end? What of the love Jesus taught? Does anyone practice this love?

We have now reached a point in history where we have huge numbers of believers that still trust the Lord Jesus, but never darken the door of the local church. At home, they read their Bible, worship to their favorite style of music, and pray with the same zeal they always have had. They may even attend the occasional conference if a special speaker is going to be in attendance. But, they can't stomach the local church and all that goes with the package.

Other wounded believers have gone the route of small house churches, and the casual environment that approach offers. The worldwide house church movement now (2006) runs around four-hundred-million believers. Once a common approach in communist China, the house church movement is now exploding in North America.

What is often the church reaction to such people? *"Back-sliders! They're backsliders I tell you! If they leave the body, they have left Jesus!"*

To my understanding, to accuse others with derogatory labels and judgments is living clearly in the Tree of the Knowledge of Good and Evil. So, who wants to attend a church that lives in death – the Tree of the Knowledge of Good and Evil? When the local church itself turns people off so much they head for the door and don't come back! Will they return if we call them derogatory names? I doubt it.

We do have a crisis in the North American church. The protestant church has looked at the Catholic church and wondered why the Catholics would stick their heads in the sand and not notice the sexual scandal developing for decades. Within the Protestant church, we have millions of people streaming out the door every year world wide, and a pastor burnout rate that exceeds over 1,000 a month in North America – yet very little is ever heard or discussed regarding this crisis. At the time of this writing there are approximately two hundred pastor care ministries working in America to slow this "closet skeleton" problem. Nearly all these ministries are poorly funded, and spend as much time trying to raise funds as they do helping the wounded leaders along the road side. They are doing their very best however, and rarely will you ever see them on the cover of Christianity Today or Charisma magazine. The dirty laundry of the church is not a popular cover-story!

It is our hope that in reading the pages of this book, you will not only be educated and encouraged, but you will be moved to join the Good Samaritan army and stop and help when everyone else is trekking down the road to their next great church activity. The challenge is a sacrificial one, often at your own expense. The Good Samaritan (Luke 10) had a destination he was headed for. He had appointments, commitments, obligations. Like the Priest and the Levite the Samaritan saw the bloody man on the side of the road. He stopped. The Good Samaritan had clean clothes and hands, but he got blood on his hands lifting the body out of the ditch. The Good Samaritan wasn't rich, but, he used his oil and bandages to help the wounded. The Good Samaritan didn't want to walk all the way to town, but he did, so the wounded man could ride his donkey. The Good Samaritan had no Visa card, but he paid for the stay at the inn for the wounded man. The Good Samaritan had a different life philosophy than the other passersby.

In the story Jesus told about the Good Samaritan, Jesus masterfully brings out the three basic philosophies of life. The robbers that jumped the man, robbed and beat the man, lived by the philosophy, "*What's yours is mine*." The religious leaders who passed by without helping because they had important ministry to do, lived by the philosophy, "*What's mine is mine*." The Good Samaritan who had all the time constraints and important commitments that anyone else had, lived by the philosophy, "*What's mine is yours*."

Which philosophy guides your life?

NOTES:

NOTES:

NOTES:

Chapter 2

Real Stories, Real Pain

There is a glorious church. Really! But humans are the current inhabitants. People do get hurt. Jesus told us offenses would come. Jesus didn't say it would reach epidemic proportions in some places like North America. Shepherds hurt the sheep. Sheep gang up and abuse the shepherd. Sheep hurt one another, and shepherds sometimes beat each other with their staves. Wolves often look on from behind the bluff and wonder about the sanity of both sheep and shepherds. Are these people nuts?

In the pages to follow we will look at what can and does happen, and explore the answer to wounding and burnout in both lay-members and church leaders.

In the stories that follow the names have been changed to protect the innocent, the guilty, the reader, the listener, and Jesus!

Nick's Story

Nick (not his real name) pastors a church that is nearly one hundred percent ethnic. Although everyone in the congregation can speak both English and the ethnic language, the congregation is divided over which language Pastor Nick should preach in. At first this is not a problem at all, but a few members keep pushing until the issue is divisive.

After many board meetings and much turmoil, it is decided

that Pastor Nick will preach in English for the first fifteen minutes of the sermon and then in the ethnic language the final fifteen minutes. The younger part of the congregation prefer the English, but the older, long time members, still have part of the sermon in the language of the "old country."

Well, Pastor Nick is a human. So sometimes he preaches sixteen minutes in English and fourteen minutes in the ethnic language. The older people then verbally attack Pastor Nick and belittle him for favoring the English preference members. Some Sundays, Pastor Nick speaks for fourteen minutes in English and sixteen minutes in the ethnic language. After the services of worship and adoration of the great God, the younger English favoring members come forward and verbally attack Pastor Nick for favoring the older ethnic members by speaking longer in the ethnic language.

The focus of the worship service is now timing Pastor Nick, to see how long he speaks in each language. The Lord Jesus nearly becomes an afterthought. Pastor Nick's weary stress-filled face speaks nothing to the congregation. The voice of his exhausted eyes is not heard. The screaming voice of Nick's slumped shoulders falls on deaf ears. Pastor Nick enters into a full blown nervous breakdown and he resigns.

It is years later, on the other side of the continent, that Kathy and I meet Pastor Nick. He recovered reasonably from his breakdown, and is now an associate pastor in a healthy church, doing visitation ministry. He is happy and content and never, ever, wants to be a senior pastor again as long as he lives.

Nick's story is not unusual. It has its own twists, but it contains many common characteristics of other stories of leader and lay member burnout. We will look at a classic story of lay member burnout in a moment, but let's first dissect Nick's story and the issues.

What happened in this church? Why would a group of grown adults push their pastor to the point of breakdown and resignation? Is not the Christian church the place the lost world looks for the very definition of love? Is not love the defining characteristic we are all to display visibly as members of His body?

Jesus Christ, the King of Kings, was not kept in first place by every member of this church. Over time, the issue of language became the most important factor in this congregation. The real leaders of the church rose up and organized “their” camps of followers and planned their strategy to win this turf war in the small congregation. Human nature began to rule rather than the gentle and loving lead of the Holy Spirit. The end result was a destroyed shepherd of God, and many disillusioned sheep. The entire congregation started living in the tree of the knowledge of good and evil, and the price for the members and the pastor was high indeed.

Brenda's Story

Brenda is a good worship leader. Her excellent music skills and charming personality are appreciated by many in the congregation. She is able to lead the group into deep worship and she adds a great deal to the overall experience. But something happens. The pastor starts picking away at her work. This begins the slow death of confidence and joy, like a cat teasing a mouse for hours. With each pastoral correction, Brenda makes changes, but it never seems enough for the pastor. The pastor is making her over into his own image. It never enters his mind that he is only god with a small g.

Even the associate pastors are finding fault with Brenda and other members of the worship team. Over the course of more than a year the worship team starts feeling overly controlled and stifled. Brenda's leadership and creativity dry and shrivel under the attack – nothing is ever good enough anymore. The rest of the worship team feels the same way.

One day the pastor approaches Brenda after services and informs her she is in rebellion for not following all of his suggestions and directives regarding the worship team. Brenda can taste the accusation like a sour lime. This projected disloyalty speaks words of death to her heart. The pastor tells her unless she is willing to apologize to the church and the entire ministry staff she should consider resignation.

Brenda goes home in total dismay. She is stunned. Several members of the worship team call that night to say they can't believe what the pastor is saying. They, too, are in shock and disbelief. Brenda doesn't know what to think. Suddenly her world of Christian love is shattered by the very leaders she is serving and following loyally. Where is God? Why is he allowing this to happen? Brenda eventually becomes deeply disillusioned and quietly drops out of church never to return. She later hears the pastor has spoken of her as a rebellious sheep because she has left their fellowship.

Brenda isn't the only sheep mistreated by an over-controlling shepherd. For some pastors, control is everything. They must be in charge and totally responsible for every speck of lint on the sanctuary carpet! When Brenda answered her call to the Lord, she thought she was entering the freedom Jesus won for her on the cross. After entering the congregation, she experienced a totally different life of manipulation and human politics dictated by the insecure pastor.

Pastor, leader and lay member alike can all experience wounding and burnout. The statistics for this affliction are staggering. By calculating the resignation numbers for leaders in a few large denominations and then projecting these numbers across the number of congregations in North

America, the resulting figure that most pastor-care ministries use is 1,000 to 1,500 pastors (leaders) a month step away from their office. Even though this is an estimated figure, stop and ponder that number for a moment.

In the liberation of Iraq, the death total for American troops hit approximately 1,000 after thirteen months of action. That same "take-out" number for church leaders occurs in the North American Church every three weeks on average!

Using the same estimated figure, one church in twenty-two forces its pastor out each year! I agree that some of these figures could be argued, but the point is, what is happening in the body of Christ is pathetic. At Smoldering Wick Ministries, I always use the 1,400 a month stat as a figure for all fallen or forced resignation leaders. So my view includes associate pastors, youth pastors, senior pastors, and even ministry leaders or teachers on a higher professional level. Here is my point: even if my broader interpretation of the 1,400 a month stat is more accurate, I don't care. The real point is, this is unacceptable. I'm sure Jesus is grieved by this horror.

At Smoldering Wick Ministries we ache with frustration because the general body of Christ keeps marching forward, never mentioning these wounded. With each turn the church makes, the ditch on each side of the road is filled with wounded, disillusioned bodies of members and former members. Our ministry and approximately two hundred other ministries like ours (in North America) are reaching out and trying to help the leaders and lay members that are needing a whole lot more than a band-aid.

Cast Out

The faded blue mini van sits covered with a thin gray coat of dust. The sunset over the campground glows with colors that reach deep inside the man and woman and remind them of things that seemed a lifetime ago. Their minds remember optimistic times in their marriage when they were filled with grand adventure, but, now, hopelessness. They remember dreams of changing the world in a better way.

Like a dying way of life, the sun slowly dips below the horizon. The sunset colors blend into the fading paint on the mini van mingling with the couple's dreams of what used to be. The two drop their eyes and start lethargically sorting the mess inside the mini van. Clothes are strewn from the front dash to the open tailgate. Each night is a challenge, arranging and re-arranging the clutter of books, clothes and personal effects for four people. Since the woman and the two children prefer to sleep inside the van, the man often curls up in a sleeping bag on the ground.

The deepening darkness feels heavy, hopeless and everlasting. The trees of the campground loom menacingly above the people like domineering figures wanting to destroy the family. The four lonely figures gather together inside the van for a prayer. The woman weeps. The children remain silent and do not pray. The man begs God for help and his voice is husky.

At the end of the prayer, the man pulls out his cell phone. "I think I will try that number again before our service is cut off."

"Hello, this is Kim Wenzel speaking."

"Hi, is this Smoldering Wick Ministries?"

"Uh, yeah, what time is it?"

"I'm sorry to call so late. We are in another time zone, and I really need to talk."

"I'm here, man, go ahead."

"Up until two weeks ago I was a pastor. It's a long story, but they finally pushed me out and demanded we move out of the parsonage immediately. No severance, no time to find new housing or another job. Now . . . now we . . . my wife and two kids, are living out of our mini van. I need some help! What do I do?" . . . sobbing.

This is not the strangest call we have received, but it is tragic and sad. This ministry family had served successfully for many years, then, the forces of human politics beat and bruised them. They were not perfect. I have never met a pastoral family that was. They have their weaknesses and idiosyncrasies, like every family I've ever met. They thought life would go on forever the way it was as a successful pastor in a denomination. It did not. The very people they had sacrificed so much for turned on them. Their best friends became their betrayers.

Jesus told us so clearly that we would participate in His sufferings. I know that is not taught much in America, but it is in your Bible. To participate in such humbling is a great thing; a life-changing experience. But it is horribly painful. What is the cost of doing nothing to help the church's wounded? What is the cost of pretending all is wonderful and bragging about the youth mission trip to South America while fellow leaders in the body of Christ fall by the side of the road and are ignored? What is the cost of doing nothing?

Fred and Jean's Story

Heavy wet clouds filled with snow and rain hang over the city of Colorado Springs completely blocking out the view of Pikes Peak. I sit down at my desk and switch on the computer. Up come the list of new e-mails and one catches my attention. A pastor in Florida wants a call from me.

"Hey Fred, this is Kim Wenzel from Smoldering Wick

Ministries in Colorado. How are you today?"

"Hi Kim. Boy it's good to hear from you. I needed to call somebody, but I didn't know who. I am at the end. I don't know what to do!"

"What happened? What is your situation?"

"Well, I had been interviewed several times by a church here in Florida. I had been pastoring in Texas, and this opportunity opened up. I received a call from one of the elders on the search committee, saying out of the final two candidates I was chosen. We (my wife and I) were both happy with this opportunity, and put our Texas house up for sale. It sold quickly, and we were off to Florida. After arriving with a U-Haul truck filled to the brim, I stopped and called the same elder for final directions to the church neighborhood. I was in for the shock of a life-time.

He laughed nervously and then said, "I am sorry, Fred, but after I talked with you, we had another meeting and decided to go with the other guy. I wish you had called earlier."

I returned to the truck to inform my wife I had no job, no church, no money, no house to live in."

"So . . . what on earth are you doing now?" I ask.

"My wife has a job and we live in an apartment. We are living week to week. I have tried to get various jobs but no luck so far. We are treading water hoping a ship comes along soon. My wife's health is not that great. If she goes down and I have no job, this could be an exciting end to our lives."

Bob's Story

Bob and Lynn enjoyed their family vacation more than usual. This was the first time Bob really let go and focused on his family. He spent extra time with Lynn, and playing with the kids in the sand on the beach really recharged Bob. He deserves an "A" for effort in that area.

They return home to Colorado, un-pack all the suitcases and equipment from the three week trip and try to relax. It was a great trip, one that Lynn, Bob's wife, wants to put into album form for lasting memories.

The next morning, Bob slowly gets started and travels to the church for some morning prayer and e-mail work. Bob walks in the door, smiles at his executive assistant as usual, and reaches for the door handle of his office. She does not smile back for the very first time. Bob nearly hurts his wrist when the door knob will not turn.

"Val, what are all these boxes doing stacked here?" Bob asks in a wondering tone.

"Pastor Bob," Val begins in a formal business-like tone, "those boxes belong to you. That is the stuff from your office."

"My office?" A horribly unfamiliar feeling travels down Bob's spine.

"Your former office."

Bob stands speechless. His eyes scan the many brown unlabeled boxes. He once again tries the doorknob to his office, this time with twice the physical effort. It will not budge.

"The lock has been changed." Val's voice starts strong and ends with a whimper. She breaks down and weeps. Immediately she jumps to her feet and runs from the room.

Bob stands alone, locked out of his office, the office of senior pastor, and all his life's work and books packed away in brown boxes sit in front of him. He stands in shock. Why? Why this way? What for? Who is the mover and the shaker of this move? Who cares? After all these years, his office was packed up while he was gone on a well deserved vacation, and now he is tossed out with no one to answer why.

Bob never returns to full time ministry.

Terry's Story

Terry is inspired by all the leadership books he reads from the local Christian book store. He is a baptized, born again Christian, wanting to do his part in furthering the Kingdom of God. At his local church, Terry hears in many sermons that all members of the church are in the ministry, and we are all part of furthering the Kingdom through our efforts. Terry is inspired by such sermons and desires to do his part. When he begins to practice such theology, the ministry leadership of the church become nervous.

"What is he doing? Terry seems very strong and influential in his teaching and leadership. Maybe we need to reel this guy in a little. He seems almost – should we say it – Charismatic! People listen to him. This could be bad. They might even follow him, God forbid."

Terry reads widely and gathers tidbits of gold from many well known Christian leaders across America. In due time the pastor approaches Terry and strongly suggests he not read certain authors because their teachings are questionable. Terry listens quietly, but continues to read widely. He begins to realize he is now in an environment at his church where he cannot speak as freely. He must think before he shares anything he learns from other radio or TV preachers or authors.

Terry continues to grow and mature as a Christian and a leader within the church, and his development is obvious to all. His ideas and understandings can no longer be hidden. He is a living testament to these truths and ideas he has studied. The conservative leadership theorizes they no longer completely control Terry and he is corrected in many subtle and not so subtle ways regarding his ideas.

As the attempts to manipulate him grow, Terry realizes the true nature of the culture within his congregation. This is not a free environment where the saved can become all Jesus has in mind. The freedom talked about in Galatians 5:1 is non-existent in his church. Terry understands the need for all to agree on the absolutes of scripture, but he wonders why people are not free to have different interpretations on the non-salvation issues. Why must he believe certain things exactly the way the pastor sees them? The more Terry looks around the congregation, the more he sees the control of puppet dictators manipulating peoples' lives in areas where they have no business. These pastors are not "helpers in your joy," but rather, small-time insecure leaders that possibly are not called to the ministry!

With each passing week, with each deeper conviction in his heart that he will not be free to develop some of his dreams, Terry moves closer to the door. One day he never comes back. Terry moves on, and launches a para-church ministry that reaches out into the community and continues to help many of the city's down and out. He eventually finds a life-giving church that allows him to fully and independently run his helpful ministry without interference.

Pastor Dean and the Death of a Church

Pastor Dean has been struggling in a small church for several years. He works very hard, but the power brokers within the membership are a source of endless hurt and criticism. The internal politics of the congregation is fatiguing everyone. Finally in sheer desperation, Dean convinces several of the denomination's leaders to come in to help resolve the tension.

The result is a shocker. After several days of listening to many members and Pastor Dean, the denominational leaders make an announcement. The denominational authority starts by reviewing the church's history within the denomination. He then discusses the current problem. Then he announces his conclusion. Because of the church's long history of broken and terminated pastors, and because the congregation is close to destroying Pastor Dean, the denomination no longer wants the congregation! The denominational leader officially closes the church, that day!

Pastor Dean finds himself immediately unemployed, and the power brokers in the congregation head off to start their own church.

Pastor Dean enters into depression and periods of time screaming at God. At the time of this writing he has never returned to full-time ministry.

Why This Book Was Written

In part 1 of this book we will explore the subject of burnout. It is not a new topic. Many of the famous in scripture experienced levels of burnout, and, like us, the experience became their breaking point leading to deeper surrender to God's will.

In part 2 of this book, we will explore the tree of life approach to walking with God. In an age of the -"what God can do for me"- gospel, you will find the tree of life approach to ministry a breath of fresh air. The gospel of Jesus Christ is Father's good news unto eternal life. The correct gospel is not a message that leads to burnout, but rather, real life. ***Burnout is characterized by a loss of hope and ideals.*** Burnout is a growing disillusionment with the church and the empty promises the church can teach. Burnout changes us forever, but if we allow Jesus to steer the experience and break down our skewed beliefs, we will emerge mature disciples, ready to teach others to walk in the tree of life and give away the very life of Father to others.

In part 3 of this book, we have a good look at how Jesus, Himself, teaches tree of life living in the Sermon on the Mount. When you understand the tree of life approach to thinking and living, Matthew 5, 6 and 7 come alive like never before!

The answer for many conflicts and stress inside the church is found in a true approach to New Covenant living. Far too many believers worship God out of the tree of the knowledge of good and evil. When both laity and leadership walk together in the tree of life, we will have churches overflowing with blood covenant love. Enjoy your reading and may the spirit of Jesus fill you to overflowing!

NOTES:

NOTES:

NOTES:

Chapter 3

Kim & Kathy's Story

The Samaritan Call

The feeling of helplessness overwhelmed me. The eyes of the dying woman stared through me. Her lifted hand trembled above her body lying in the gutter. She was dying before my eyes and I was dying inside. The world was ending for both of us. But let me start at the beginning.

Growing up in Western Canada, I spent my free time climbing mountains and skiing. The joy of Canadian prosperity and endless freedom I took for granted. I enjoyed the vast wilderness and the newness of all the cities. My friends and I never gave much thought to other parts of the world and other living conditions. We did our thing, trekking down the road to our Jericho, enjoying the lives of ski bums and mountaineers. We had our dreams and priorities, and little care for others.

After high school, I began a lifestyle of hitch-hiking around the world. I would work in the home construction industry for six months, pocket all the money, and then head overseas to explore the world, and, of course, continue my climbing career. The West coast of North America and Europe became my playground. We would sleep in tents, or under picnic tables, travel, climb, ski, backpack and explore with little agenda other than high adventure.

After five years of such a nomadic lifestyle, the heavy questions of life and purpose awakened deep in the hiding places of my heart. It never works to suppress this spirit. When the Holy Spirit starts to knock and seek your heart, it's impossible to pretend He isn't there. In my reading and questioning of life, I came across an article based on Acts 2:38: Repent, be baptized, and receive the Holy Spirit. The life changing article impacted me, but I already planned a wild journey through Southern Africa, and within days I was winging my way to the far side of the earth.

After five weeks of hitchhiking and sight seeing, my body is in Salisbury, Rhodesia, and the Holy Spirit is still tapping my shoulder and playing games with my heart. My mind is in Salisbury also, but it is not content with the nomadic hippy life anymore. The Holy Spirit is gaining ground on me, and I can't ignore Him much longer. The next day would bring the event that changed my life forever.

I stumble out of my one-star hotel mid-morning and start on a pleasant little walk through the streets of Salisbury. Well, it starts pleasantly. Funny how we don't know when our life is going to end. I have no clue I am living the last few minutes of my life. Death can be around the next corner, waiting for you, while the Holy Spirit smiles in anticipation.

Turning a corner, I start down the street, looking in shop windows, and enjoying a bit of sun. I wheel to my right to cross the street, and I suddenly enter "the twilight zone." In front of me, in the gutter, across the street, lies a body. As I approach, the African lady opens her eyes and starts raising her hand toward me. Her hand is merely skin stretched over bone. Her eyes hold no life, like a cancer patient just moments before death. She cries out to me in a pitiful voice, barely audible. My stomach knots and hair on my neck stands at attention.

I glance right and left. The street in both directions is completely vacant. No living soul, visible or heard, but the dying lady and myself. Again she whispers. The language I can not understand, but the pain and nearness of death I do understand. Life is leaving her and she is crying out to me for help. But, what can I do? I am young, inexperienced, with no training in life saving. I know nothing of her beliefs, or how to comfort her as she enters the great beyond. The profound feeling of being useless overwhelms me. The African lady is dying, and my life of self-focus and self-fulfillment starts to die with her. Another wave of helplessness and uselessness swoons over me like a hot flash. In sheer desperation I reach into my pocket, and pull out a piece of money. I place the coin in the dying woman's hand. She looks at the coin and her lifeless eyes look up into mine. She does not speak. Her eyes say it all. The coin is of no value to her.

Then . . . I turn and walk away . . . .

I just turn and walk away. Overwhelmed, I simply walk away from a dying person on the side of the road. I have never been the same since. To this day her eyes still haunt me. I think no one should ever have to walk away from a dying person. Part of you dies with them. But, as the years roll by, I am surprised. Some have no problem walking away and letting others die in the ditch. Jesus tells a great story about just that!

I returned home to Canada from Africa, attended Bible College, married and launched into a ministry career that is now in it's twenty-ninth year. Around the twenty year mark, I was fired by the legalistic denomination I served because I was teaching far too much grace and faith and associating with "other" churches and pastors. When Kathy and I were tossed out, we started to experience the "side of the road" syndrome. Friends and fellow pastors we chatted with over the phone and email suddenly disappeared off the face of the earth. Kathy and I suddenly had leprosy. We were deeply hurt, wounded and bleeding, yet, our friends walked away. Oh, what a feeling.

We remained in Canada another three years pastoring a small independent church, then, made the move to Colorado Springs to be part of New Life Church. Pastor Ted Haggard had befriended us and even spoken in our tiny independent church in Ontario. I became part of the small group ministry at New Life Church, and Kathy worked with the home school association.

Everywhere we went in Colorado Springs, fast food restaurants, gasoline stations, stores, we kept meeting former pastors who were still hurting. Their stories all had common denominators. They admitted they made their fair share of mistakes. They were all shocked how merciless the church could be. They were all totally abandoned after termination. They all knew what it felt like to be left dying on the side of the road.

Inspired by the Holy Spirit, Kathy and I decided to launch a ministry to help burned out and wounded church leaders. We realized somebody has to stop and help the bleeding and wounded if the church is going to keep trekking on to Jerusalem. But where do we begin?

We named it Smoldering Wick Ministries, started a web site, and wondered if anyone would ever find our ministry. In less than a week, we were receiving four to six e-mails a day from pastors all over the world. We were shocked!

One day the Holy Spirit simply impacted me with what Father was up to in my life. Three decades before, I had walked away from a dying lady on the side of the road. Then I had no training, skill, experience, poise. Now, I had what I needed. Decades of experience as a church pastor, the experiences of hurt, wounding, rejection, attack, slander, termination and being left to die on the road side myself. Now, I can reach out and help with skill and experience, those abandoned on the side of the road!

In my calling, the Holy Spirit engineered an experience that changed my life forever back in Africa. At the time I had no idea He was preparing me for a ministry that would not launch for three more decades. But, here we are now, with a 30 acre retreat ranch for burned out pastors, youth pastors, worship leaders, even church members who feel burnt by the body.

The church continues to march onward to Jericho or Jerusalem, leaving behind over one thousand pastors a month (in North America) – men and women who are lying in the ditch with black eyes and bleeding hearts. More than thirty years ago I walked away from a dying lady on the roadside. I can't walk away again. I am shocked how easily the church does it, every day, every month, and every year.

After a quarter century of pastoring, I don't even have the desire to get to Jerusalem or Jericho. Something tells me if I spend my time out here in no man's land, picking up the wounded, and loving them with blood covenant love, I may end up meeting Jesus sooner than some might think.

NOTES:

NOTES:

NOTES:

Chapter 4

Elijah in his Cave

"Elijah was a man just like us. He prayed earnestly that it would not rain, and it did not rain on the land for three and a half years. Again he prayed, and the heavens gave rain, and the earth produced its crops." (NIV James 5:17)

Elijah is certainly a prophet of God. God works many miracles through this man and makes him a spokesman of His will. An awesome witness of God's power is displayed involving Elijah on Mt. Carmel. The prophets of Baal are destroyed and the nation of Israel is stunned. Yet, Elijah plummets into depression right after the prophets of Baal are destroyed.

What kind of expectations does Elijah have in the wake of the Mt. Carmel shootout?

Have you ever pondered what has caused you the greatest, or, at least a major heartache? Was it really someone else, or something else? How much did your unfulfilled expectations play a role in your disappointment? Who gave you those expectations? Why did those shattered expectations have such an impact on your heart? Why do the sharp jagged edges of a shattered dream cut so deeply?

Back to Elijah's shootout at the Mt. Carmel corral: the prophets of Baal and Asherah are defeated. The whole nation now knows that Yahweh is the true God. Yet, in the eyes of one man, Elijah, nothing has changed. He can't see it. He knows not what is happening deep in people's hearts across the nation. His focus ties in with *his expectation,* not God's expectation! Elijah sees through a pair of sunglasses tinted the color of *his* dream. The Great Revival *he* expected has not started. The world has not been turned upside down. Through the eyes of Elijah, everything remains the same.

Elijah's heart is heavy; his mind confused. It has been a day on Mt. Carmel to remember and tell your grandchildren about. It was a day when the very presence of God showed up in power and authority. Many live and die wishing for such an experience. Elijah saw it and participated in the events. Yet, he is left empty. Unsatisfied. Incomplete. Agitated. What did he expect? How soon did he expect it? What would it look like when *his expectation* came to pass?

Later he hears from Jezebel, the queen herself, still alive and still in charge, still promoting Baal worship in the nation. She declares that she will kill Elijah. Elijah is discouraged, and tumbles into a state of depression, often called burnout by some of us.

Elijah's first reaction was to run away. Stop fighting the system. Life isn't working. The results he expected from God did not materialize. Why die for a cause that seems to be failing? This did not mean he himself had lost all belief and faith in God. He certainly did not. But his dream of unprecedented revival did not materialize. Not only that, but it seems as if nothing at all has changed after the great work on Mt. Carmel! Nothing!

Elijah heads for the desert: the wilderness; the place of nature, where mankind isn't. The easiest thing to do is sleep. It doesn't hurt when you are unconscious. But, before he falls asleep, he prays that he might die.

When you are in the state of burnout, you don't always think rationally or logically. If Elijah really wanted to die, he could have simply stayed put, and Jezebel would have killed him! When our dreams are shattered, our emotions exhausted, and our mind weary, we often are *illogical* and *irrational*. It's OK. We're in good company. Many of us have been there.

The angels of God take care of Elijah, feeding him and watching out for him. God does not forsake the burned out, ever. He continues to pursue and love and look after those who deeply love Him. Elijah is in the midst of an inner war, and he comes up with a reason to make sense of it all.

"I have been very zealous for the LORD God Almighty. The Israelites have rejected your covenant, broken down your altars, and put your prophets to death with the sword. I am the only one left, and now they are trying to kill me too." (NIV 1 Kings 19:13).

It is so very hard to serve God with all your being and then feel that your efforts guided by God have come to nothing. It reveals how much of the old man still lives in us; that old man that should die daily. The human spirit has to deal with this apparently unfruitful effort somehow. Often we will stumble into the tree of the knowledge of good and evil and blame someone else. At this point Elijah is willing to reject the entire nation and blame them for not responding to the power display at Mt. Carmel. His memorized complaint ends with the comment that he, too, was going to be killed. Self-pity often manifests when we are burned out and feeling useless despite our service to God.

Over the course of this forty day wilderness trip, God never becomes angry, nor does he scold Elijah. God is with him, but allows the process to run its course to prepare Elijah for the truth to come.

Elijah enters a cave on the mountain and sleeps the night. The next day God speaks to him for the first time and asks, "What are you doing here, Elijah?"

Elijah repeats his memorized statement; *"I have been very zealous for the LORD God Almighty. The Israelites have rejected your covenant, broken down your altars, and put your prophets to death with the sword. I am the only one left, and now they are trying to kill me too."* (NIV I Kings 19:13).

God says, "Go out and stand on the mountain in the presence of the Lord, for the Lord is about to pass by."

Elijah does as he is told, and then a great display of power unfolds. A mighty wind so strong it tears the mountain open, shattering rocks and boulders in front of Elijah. Elijah is intimidated. Next, a great earth quake that seems to shake the whole earth. Every cell in Elijah's body trembles. An electrical fire storm erupts that surpasses anything Elijah has ever seen. The very smell of lightening fills the air. Yet, through all this magnificent power display, Elijah does not see God. God said he was going to pass by, but all Elijah sees is great power.

Elijah stands still in the profound silence that follows. His senses numb from mega-sensory bombardment. Then he hears it: a quiet whisper, a faint voice gently speaking into his heart and spirit. Elijah is drawn to the cave mouth where he hears the voice.

"Elijah . . . what are you doing here?" whispers the presence of God.

"I have been very zealous for the LORD God Almighty. The Israelites have rejected your covenant, broken down your altars, and put your prophets to death with the sword. I am the only one left, and now they are trying to kill me too," Elijah replies.

"Go back the way you came," is God's reply. God gives him his new assignments regarding who to anoint, and then God states the fact that at least seven thousand others in the nation are loyal and faithful to Him. Elijah is not alone in his zeal and commitment to God.

Reality starts to dawn on Elijah. Like the first color changes of the eastern sky at dawn, the light of reality slowly and steadily fills Elijah's intellect. Great power displays *do not* change hearts. Elijah, himself, has just witnessed the greatest power display of his lifetime, and when asked what he is doing here, he just repeats the same old, same old. The great power Elijah has just seen has not changed his heart or attitude. Elijah begins to understand that it is the sweet whisper of God's love and patience that has turned his heart, not raw power. As he ponders this fact it dawns on Elijah that perhaps this same conclusion can be reached with the Mt. Carmel power show. The true God is revealed at Mt. Carmel, but few hearts have *visibly* turned. Mt. Carmel had its purpose, but real revival in Israel will occur through the sweet whisper of God's voice into each spirit in the people, from the inside out, not outside in.

Elijah starts recovering from burnout and disillusionment the instant he starts to see God in a *new and more accurate way*. God is not forcing anyone to do anything. He was and still is whispering into the hearts and spirits of people, loving them toward the Kingdom.

Our expectations of people and what *we* want them to do can be a source of deep hurt and disappointment. Power displays from the pulpit will not work, but love from God will. Elijah learns to ***relax*** and leave the plan of God to God. He can and will work it out. Elijah's expectations after this event are more realistic.

After this burnout experience, Elijah goes back to work, and neither God nor Elijah ever mention Mt. Carmel again. Elijah's ministry empowers other prophets who rise up to preach God's word to the King of Israel and the Israelites. Elijah doesn't take it personally when other people fail to obey God, as he did before. He is more settled in his faith and trust that God will actually finish what he starts no matter what other people do. *This frees Elijah to serve God without worrying about the response of others.* He is no longer repeating the memorized message to God. His burnout leads to a new relationship with God.

NOTES:

NOTES:

NOTES:

Chapter 5

David at Ziklag

Pastor George had been on one of his marathon visits to the elderly and hospitalized members of his congregation. Two of his dear ladies were in the hospital dying from cancer and he was trying to make sense of their suffering while giving encouragement to them and to their families. One elderly man was having trouble with his adult son taking advantage of him and needed counsel on what measures to take to reconcile. Two families were involved in turmoil over their teenage children being caught in compromising circumstances together. The week had been full of crisis calls and ongoing trials. Pastor George had felt a gnawing pain in his abdomen for several days in a row and thought he might have to get a doctor's appointment for next week. As he neared the church for the regular monthly board meeting he prayed for the peace of God upon himself. He knew that there were some unresolved issues that would be brought up.

He was not prepared for what he met at that meeting. Three of the board members met him at the door looking grim. As he entered the room he immediately recognized the denominational bishop for the area and reached out to shake his hand. He only received a cold glance from the bishop which sent a chill up George's spine. Two of Pastor George's most loyal friends patted him on the back and asked how he was. Then the meeting was called to order. As the minutes were read Pastor George glanced around the room and wondered what was going on. There was such a serious note in everyone's voice that his heart began to pound within him. What has happened? He found out as soon as new business was brought up. The Board was not happy with his inability to minister to every sector of the congregation, namely the children and young families. They were ready to send him packing while they looked for a new pastor. Pastor George did not know what to say. He had not seen this coming. He was speechless and his emotional fatigue would not even allow him to defend himself. Heartsick and feeling totally alone, he cried out, "Lord God, what is happening to me?"

If you are like me you have experienced times of great fatigue, combined with mental and emotional exhaustion. The ministry can take you there rapidly. People who serve the public in critical areas experience it, doctors, nurses, teachers, small business owners. When this occurs on a frequent basis we can become so disillusioned with the church and with people that we seriously consider resigning.

We are not alone. David and many others experienced the same testing, and David leaves us a wonderful example to follow.

David and his men had been riding for three days to get home to Ziklag. The last few miles of any journey seem the longest, as you anticipate seeing your wife and children again, and sinking your teeth into a good home-cooked meal for the first time in ages. Their saddle sores were hurting, and their legs ached with stiffness as the men rode those last few miles over the hill tops.

Suddenly someone shouted, "Smoke!" All eyes lifted to the horizon, the deep grey plume twisted skyward and to the left as the breeze carried it. Every man knew Ziklag was over the next hill, and they urged their horses to quicken the pace. As each rider crested the hill, it only required one glance before they kicked their horses into a gallop toward the burning city. Adrenalin surged through the men's veins as they thought of their families and friends. Who had done such a thing, and were they still looting the town?

The thunder of hooves mixed with the crackle of the dying flames as the men rode into town with swords drawn. Within minutes they realized they were nearly the only ones in town. The wives and children had been taken. Each exhausted rider slumped into despair, rummaging through the dwelling their family had occupied. With family, valuables and mementoes all missing, the deep hurt of having the heart cut out settled on each man. Hurt so deep it caused blood to boil.

The weeping lasted until each man neared total fatigue, yet something in each man cried out for some kind of action. All the sacrifice they had made to serve with David no longer seemed worth the cost. All the endless days they had spent away from wives and children. The dangers of the battles they fought, and the constant running and hiding. The price had been high, and now with this disaster, the men grew insanely angry. In turn each man bent down and picked up a stone large enough to kill.

David's stress chart now peaked well above "normal." In his exhaustion and infinitely deep wounding and pain how was he to handle being stoned to death by his own men in the next five minutes? Well, did he go away for three days of fasting and prayer? I guess the five minute situation cancelled that plan. The immediacy of the moment also ruled out a half dozen counseling sessions with a $200 an hour therapist. Ziklag isn't near Colorado, so a week-end get-away at Vail with a hot tub was out of the question. How about sitting down and studying ten chapters of the scripture? No, that would take more than five minutes. Even a two hour prayer gathering with everyone laying hands on David and blessing him with protection was out of the question. God placed David in a situation where every one of our modern answers would not do the trick.

With no time, no energy, and no credibility left, what did David do? 1 Samuel 30:6 says, "*But David found strength in the Lord his God.*" How? By remembering *who* lived inside of him. By remembering *who* anointed him to be the next King of Israel. By remembering *who* had given him and his descendants promises and by remembering *what* those promises were. Was God about to allow all those promises to fail because of a group of exhausted hurting men? Not a chance. David reminded himself of these things and remembered *whose* spirit lived inside of him and realized even this completely hopeless situation was going to work out just fine.

David talked with Abiathar the priest to receive the counsel of God, and God said pursue the Amalekites. David redirected his men's anger toward the true enemy, and when they caught up with the raiding party it was lights out for the Amalekites.

David gives us several key ideas in this true story. First, the answer lies within us, yet not of us, but of God himself. The answer is not in "things" we should do. Please don't misunderstand what I am saying. Prayer, Bible study, fasting, all are basic disciplines of the Christian walk. Yet, none replace the Holy Spirit inside us and listening to His lead. The answer is not in what *we should do*, but rather in what *God has done* and promised us. Please beware of "religion" and things you *should do* so that God will do this and that.

Also, we find in the account of the story, two hundred men who were simply too exhausted to carry on, and when the battle was won against the Amalekites, some wanted the exhausted left out of receiving the spoils of the battle. David disagreed. Those who maintained and held on to what ground has been gained receive the same reward. All shared. All got their families back, and their share of the spoils. At Smoldering Wick we realize and totally accept the fact that some burned out church leaders are not able to continue the battle in the ministry. They drop out and do what they can in a supportive role like David's two hundred men. We do not judge or condemn them. We bless them as David did and we love them and help everyone to draw near to God.

In your life and mine, there will be many Ziklags. Places and circumstances where all we can do will never ever be enough; places and circumstances where we are totally fried mentally, emotionally and even spiritually; places and circumstances where all of our education and experience will not help us; places and circumstances where every one of our good friends turn on us or disappear; places and circumstances where remembering who lives in us is our only recourse. We can turn only to one solution, the flow of God's grace. It is here, to this twilight zone, that Jesus is calling us in Matt. 11:27-30. It is here, finally, that we give up on methodology, and *learn to rest in his spirit.*

May all be blessed and healed by the great God and His wonderful son, Jesus.

NOTES:

NOTES:

NOTES:

Chapter 6

Asaph's Wake up Call

King David brings the Ark of the Covenant back to Jerusalem. What a wonderful exciting time in the history of the nation. We think our World's Fairs and Olympic games are high times, but for Israel, having the very Ark of the Covenant back in Jerusalem was almost unbelievable for that generation of followers. What excitement, what joy, what a time when young and old smiled with hope and optimism!

David chose three worship leaders to lead the nation each day in worship of the great YHVH. One of those worship leaders was named Asaph. If the name sounds familiar it is because he wrote several Psalms that are included in scripture.

In Psalm 73, we have his story of burnout and disillusionment. It is a classic. Each day Asaph led the nation in grand worship, and no doubt he felt his job was important. Most of the time, Asaph probably enjoyed the worship ministry. What a blessing!

But something started to bother him. Asaph's spirit started to sour.

As the days and weeks rolled by, he noticed many people in the nation were prosperous and having an easier time with life than he himself. Asaph tried humbly to lead worship, and expected a certain level of blessing to come his way for carrying out such an important job. After all, is this not one of the greatest ministries in the history of the nation? Of course it is, Asaph probably thought.

But as he walked through life, it seemed in Asaph's reasoning, the proud and wicked enjoyed the things he wanted to enjoy. After seeing this repeatedly, Asaph started deceiving himself into believing there was no value to serving the great God. The blessings of God are just rhetoric, he probably thought. Asaph reached a point he believed the wicked were always carefree and increasing in wealth (Psalm 73:12).

Time marches on and Asaph feels so strongly about this apparent injustice he seriously considers speaking his complaints publicly and possibly resigning as worship leader (ever been there?). Thankfully Asaph realizes to speak such things will mislead the children of God and that would be a betrayal. He ponders these matters until he feels so oppressed and disillusioned he is beside himself. The more he tries to figure it out by his human reasoning, the more confused and depressed he becomes.

The loving God stepped in as he did with Elijah, as he did with David, as he did with Saul of Tarsus, as he does for everyone he humbles, and he reaches out to Asaph in the sanctuary. How ironic! Asaph's ministry is in the sanctuary, leading the people in worship of the great God, yet somehow, Asaph had never entered into deep relationship with this same God himself! He had been so busy leading others to God, he forgot to have a connection himself! God shows up in the sanctuary, and Asaph begins to see a bigger picture.

As Asaph's relationship with God grows he comes to understand that life isn't always what you see with the eye. The wicked are not always enjoying everything the rest of us would love to have – money, free time, good health. Asaph came to read between the lines regarding the plan of God, and understood the here and now is not the end of the story.

Asaph had made the treasure of his heart something other

than relationship with the great God. Asaph had expectations for himself that were different than God's, and led to that magnificent emotional state called *disillusionment*.

The relationship with God was not the number one passion of Asaph's heart, even though he was involved in heartfelt worship everyday! Incredible, yet it happens all the time with ministry leaders.

Let all of us worship God with all our being, yet, let us never forget that even worship does not replace relationship! Worship is part of relationship. In the end, Asaph looks to God as his refuge, not money or materialism (verse 28).

NOTES:

NOTES:

NOTES:

Chapter 7

Hannah's Heartbreak

Little Hannah grew up in a nation where people had freedom to live and worship as they chose. There were occasional wars and sometimes great oppression from other nations. Great heroes rose up from time to time and helped free the people from their enemies. Most people did what they thought was right and the only national leader was an old priest who sat in the tabernacle at Shiloh and talked to people when they came to sacrifice to God.

Hannah planned to have a large family and be a joyful mother and wife. She understood the power that she would wield as a mother training up her children to live within the Law of God. Israel was called to be a model nation and Hannah was going to be a model mother to educate the next generation. It was her dream and her calling.

When Hannah married she was blessed with a godly man, named Elkanah. But for some reason he married another woman, too. As years passed, Hannah failed to get pregnant and the other woman, Peninnah, had many children. This was a painful situation that affected Hannah every day of her life. Her very reason for living was not happening!

But every year the whole family kept the law God had given to Moses and went up to the tabernacle in Shiloh to worship and to present sacrifices. When sacrifices were made a portion of the meat was given to Peninnah and to her sons and daughters, but Elkanah gave a double portion to Hannah, because he loved her, *and the Lord had closed her womb.* It seems that Elkanah had looked at the situation and concluded that it was the Lord who had closed Hannah's womb. There were precedents to this: Sarah, Rebecca and Rachel, foremothers of the nation of Israel, had all experienced the sorrow of childlessness.

Not everyone in the family accepted this childlessness. Peninnah, known as "the rival", "provoked her in order to irritate her". She sounds like some people I know who love to provoke others to anger. They just like to get "a rise" out of others. There are even people like this is churches. Little do they know what great sorrow they are bringing to their fellows or even to their families. They find the great sore spot in a person's life and peck at it like chickens do when they dislike one in the flock. Chickens can peck at another chicken until it dies of its injuries. People can peck at people until great damage is done.

As the account says, "This went on year after year". How long did Hannah have to endure not only her childlessness but also the chiding of her rival? Year after year while the other woman produced child after child. "Whenever Hannah went up to the house of the Lord her rival provoked her till she wept and would not eat. Elkanah her husband would say to her, 'Hannah, why are you weeping? Why don't you eat? Why are you downhearted? Don't I mean more to you than ten sons?" He seemed to know what was bothering her but couldn't stop the other woman from destroying Hannah whom he loved.

For most of us the trial we must bear is enough. We may be able to bear it, but the ridicule of others around us is what really causes us to fall apart. We need compassion, tenderness and mercy from others, not their judgment or superiority. We are judging ourselves enough and the devil is continually accusing us. We don't need the pointing finger, the crude jokes, and laughter behind our backs. We don't need to be comparing ourselves to others. This is not wisdom.

Hannah endured this trial for many years but one day, when she had finished eating and drinking in Shiloh, she stood up! She had had enough! She stood up. She decided to do something about this situation. The whole family looked at her in astonishment. Did she go over and punch Peninnah's nose? Did she decide to walk out of the family? NO!

"In bitterness of soul Hannah wept much and prayed to the Lord. And she made a vow saying, 'O Lord Almighty, if you will only look upon your servant's misery and remember me, and not forget your servant but give her a son, then I will give him to the Lord for all the days of his life, and no razor will ever be used on his head.'" Hannah was weeping before the Lord as she may have done many times.

The thing that was different about this time was the presence of a man anointed by God to minister to the people. Eli, the priest, observed her praying in her heart, with only her lips moving and he immediately came to conclusion that she was drunk. His first reaction to her was another accusation and reprimand. He said, "How long will you keep on getting drunk? Get rid of your wine."

Poor Hannah, the minister was accusing her now! But she replied, "Not so, my lord. I am a woman who is **deeply troubled**. I have not been drinking wine or beer. I was pouring out my soul to the Lord. Do not take your servant for a wicked woman, I have been praying here out of **my great anguish and grief**."

Here Eli speaks words of life to Hannah, "Go in peace, and may the God of Israel grant you what you have asked of him." The good news! Hannah took those words and ran with them. You can see how these words reached her heart in the next verse: "Then she went her way and ate something and **her face was no longer downcast**."

Hannah had dealt with her trial and had wallowed in her

misery for a long time. She was miserable because she couldn't give birth to a new life and she was miserable because other people saw the lack of productivity and blamed her for her problem. Yet, it was God who had closed her womb. It was God who was waiting for the right time to give her a son! It was God who knew when to open her womb. When the time was right he placed Eli, the priest, where he could see her so that he could speak words of life into the situation. Wow! Did Eli even know how God was using him? He probably did not until Samuel was brought to the tabernacle to live.

In a short time after Elkanah's family returned home Hannah became pregnant. When the child was born she named him Samuel, saying, "Because I asked the Lord for him." Of course, she was careful to fulfill her vow concerning his upbringing, and no razor touched his head. He was a Nazarite. She was also careful to nurse him and teach him and provide the best for him. She gave him to God as soon as he was weaned (which was probably at around three or four years old, not six months of age.)

When Hannah brought Samuel to the tabernacle she said, "I prayed for this child, and the Lord has granted me what I asked of him. So now I give him to the Lord. For his whole life he will be given over to the Lord." And he worshipped the Lord there. Next you can read Hannah's prayer to the Lord when she dedicated her son to the Lord. It is in I Samuel 2. Hannah was willing to give up her only son just as she had promised because now she had a reason to live. She had produced. She had fulfilled the call on her life. She could be content.

She went home, visited her son every year and gave him a new robe that she had made for him. "*And the Lord was gracious to Hannah; she conceived and gave birth to three sons and two daughters. Meanwhile the boy Samuel grew up in the presence of the Lord*".

Have you sorrowed over situations that were not productive? Have you been longing to give birth to something big but been unable to do so? What is the longing of your heart that the devil is accusing and ridiculing about? Is it time for the minister of God to speak agreement with your prayer? Let us pray this together.

May the God of Abraham, Isaac and Jacob grant you what you have asked of him!

NOTES:

NOTES:

NOTES:

Chapter 8

Answer in Emmaus

It is a time of total emptiness. Exhausted; stretched beyond your previous limits; your body, mind and spirit are bathing in the aftermath of something so demanding it has taken nearly everything out of you. Your body is trembling and your mind is totally disoriented, like being drugged or intoxicated, yet, without ever taking a drink. Your mind feels numb, and you have trouble thinking clearly. You are walking around in a fog of disbelief and shock.

That was the state of two disciples when they began their walk down the road that led to the small town of Emmaus.

What had happened, they asked themselves over and over again? They could remember the events of the past three days in Jerusalem. Those events were crystal clear, yet, nothing had been as they expected. What did they believe? How did they come to believe what they did? How could they be so wrong? Why were they so convinced of what they previously believed? They had been so certain. Now . . . now what?

As the first steps of the journey began, the two were not certain where exactly they were going. Perhaps back fishing? Maybe. If that were the case, it would be simply putting in time. The big dream was over. The great plans cancelled. The hopes and excitement dashed like waves on the rocks of Galilee's west shore. Fishing and carpentry would now be nothing more than a living. A task to be done until death came visiting. The chores to do, the taxes to pay and the Romans to put up with; that was all. Just surviving in this life like every body else.

The two men began to discuss with growing openness how they felt deep inside, finding some comfort in each other. As they spoke they were joined by a third man, who listened to their heartache for a time. The third man heard the pain and inner turmoil. The third man felt their disillusionment, and bewilderment. The third man realized the two were burned out in their spirits. The third man saw the two had lost their hope and their dreams.

The third man begins to speak. He tells stories from the Hebrew Bible. He walks the two disciples through the prophetic teachings about the Messiah, and all that would happen to him. Story by story, sentence by sentence, word by word the third man starts to rebuild understanding and even hope into the two men. As the bewildered, emotionally exhausted men listen, the importance of accurate understanding of the Messiah becomes clear. Their burned out hearts and shattered dreams become the doorway through which the third man reveals the true understanding of the Messiah. With their dreams now blown away, they begin to see with new eyes what God is truly doing.

The trio reaches the town of Emmaus, the town with the name that means "hot bath." The two disciples were having their minds and hearts bathed clean of misunderstandings and inaccurate expectations. They were being warmed and soothed by the truth and the correct Gospel of God's plan through the Messiah.

They asked the third man to stop and eat with them. They persisted, and he agreed. After finding a place to eat, they all sat down and broke bread. Only those present could tell us exactly how the next events unfolded, but we all wish for such an experience. As they talked and broke bread, the two came to see the truth in a crystal clear manner, and instantly saw the third man for who he really was, Jesus the risen Christ!

Jesus then disappears back to Jerusalem, and the two men head back down the seven mile road to Jerusalem themselves to share their news and new understanding. The healing of their burnout and total despair has started, and they have new strength and new hope that carries them joyfully up the seven mile road. Seeing Jesus with new and true eyes is what made the difference. Having a whole new relationship with Jesus, based on Jesus' dreams, not their own, made all the difference. A new and correct understanding of the Gospel is what made the difference.

No, they didn't change their diet. No, they didn't delegate more. No, they didn't exercise more. No they didn't take an extra day off every week. No, they didn't go away to the mountains and fast and pray for three days. No, they didn't go off to a resort and sit in a hot tub and unwind for a week. All the modern day answers for burnout are not what healed these two men. A new experience with Jesus is what started the healing. After . . . after all their dreams, incorrect hopes and understandings were shattered and blown to bits, they were treated to a clear accurate view of Jesus, and a new relationship with him. Thank God for burnout! It hurts like hell, but it keeps us out of hell!

NOTES:

NOTES:

NOTES:

Chapter 9

Paul's Wake up Call

God has his definition of success and greatness. Man has another. The two are a long way apart and headed in opposite directions. Yet, sometimes one can seem like the other. Man's definition can disguise itself to look like God's. A man can get caught up in man's definition of success, right and wrong, and greatness, fully believing he is seeking God's definition.

Such a man was Saul of Tarsus. He was born a Roman citizen, born a Jew and educated at the foot of Gamaliel. He rose up through the ranks of extreme legalism in the religious system of the day. He climbed the ladder. He had the clothes. He had the titles. He had the wit. He had the wisdom. Saul of Tarsus was a big-shot. He was the cover photo on the latest issue of Pharisees Today Magazine. His conferences on Fence Laws were always sold out!

Saul was disturbed by this new movement called Christianity. They were a threat. They seemed so free and loving, they could not know God. Besides, they preached pure heresy – a crucified Messiah – outrageous! He decided to wipe them out. One day, while this self appointed bounty hunter was out tracking down Christians, he decided to head toward Damascus.

What is it like experiencing devastating shock? What is it like to find out what you always assumed – no, were rock solid convinced was true – is not? What is it like when the anchors of your life fail, and you find yourself adrift? I well remember the day I came home after visiting church members in our congregation in Ontario, and my wife Kathy met me at the door and informed me my father had died of a heart attack. My dad was the first to go, so the shock of a parent death hit me. But, an even bigger shock hit!

Kathy and I flew out to Edmonton, Alberta, to perform the funeral, and we stayed with my mother. The day after our arrival in Edmonton the three of us went down to dad's bank to get his will from the safety deposit box. The very kind bank manager was writing down a list of all the contents of the safety deposit box for our lawyer, when she stopped, and handed me a small envelope.

"Here, Kim, you can have this. It's marked personal."

I opened the envelope and found a short note written in my dad's shaky handwriting. "Dear Kim, by the time you read this note, I will be dead. I think you should know, *I'm not your real father*."

Losing your dad is tough. Losing your dad twice in the same week is a bit much.

He did say a few other things and wished me a happy life, but, the shock of his first statement left my head spinning. For forty-two years I had no reason to doubt who my dad was. For forty-two years I called him dad and he called me Kim. Suddenly, all that I had understood regarding my family flew out the window. A hundred questions entered my mind, none had answers. When I stood up at the funeral home to deliver the message, I looked out over a crowd of aging sober faces. What did they know? Did they know who my dad was? Who knew the truth and who was walking around in an illusion like I had been?

Four years later we returned to Edmonton to perform my mother's funeral. Guess what we found out? No, I was not adopted. But as we cleaned house we found my Mother's government application form for the widow's pension. We discovered my parents were never married! My mother had worn a wedding ring, and used my father's name for forty-two years, but they had simply lived common law. I can not describe to you the wild twist your mind takes when you find out such things. All those innocent days growing up and having fun and laughing and playing and doing things with my parents, and now I find out what I had anchored that part of my life to was a lie. Some of you readers can relate. You have your stories to tell also.

Saul traveled the road to Damascus feeling good about himself. He was developing a reputation as a strong leader who would never compromise with the religion of Israel. His name and fame were growing. That fame would spread even more after all the Christian trash was cleaned out of Damascus. Then it happened: the shock of a lifetime; the unthinkable.

A bright light shot out of heaven so strong, it blinded Saul. In an instant Mr. Big Shot was lying on the ground, weak, blind and scared out of his wits. In an instant Saul had gone from totally self-managed, self-sufficient, to utterly helpless. Next, Saul heard the voice. The voice Saul never believed existed. The voice of a peasant Galilean carpenter who became a crucified Messiah. The voice of the resurrected Jesus. Saul's head started spinning so fast he nearly had whiplash.

"Saul, Saul, why are you persecuting me?"

"Who are you Lord," Saul's voice trembled like it never had before.

"I am Jesus, whom you are persecuting. It is hard to kick against the goads."

Saul, then in a state of shock that leaves him almost speechless sputtered, "Lord, what do you want me to do?" Those very words sounded strange to Saul's own ears. He never ever imagined he would say such a thing to a Messiah he did not believe in. It all seemed so surreal to Saul. How could this be? This was unthinkable according to everything he had ever been taught and knew.

"Arise and go into the city, and you will be told what you must do," replied the voice of Jesus.

Saul lay on the ground, in a world of complete darkness. Silence now reigned. All the people with Saul stood speechless. They had heard the voice, yet saw nothing, and they, too, were trembling. After a long time, Saul slowly, on shaky legs, got to his feet, and announced to his party he could not see. He was blind. With no one having much to say, two friends held each arm of Saul, and in silence they made their way down the remaining miles to the city of Damascus.

The impact of the experience was taking its toll on Saul. He repeatedly asked himself how this could be. How could he have been so wrong? Can the majority of the teachers of Israel be in error? The only conclusion was yes, but it seemed so shocking that the majority could be wrong. Yet, it must be. A whole religious system many hundreds of years old was off track and in error, misleading thousands. Amazing! Practices, traditions, and understandings all skewed. Leading men, famous for their preaching, all misleading people in their own ignorance! Incredible! The vast majority can be wrong, very wrong indeed! Saul's mind was overloaded and bursting with shock and bewilderment.

For three days Saul was beside himself, not eating a thing. For three long days he lived in a world of physical darkness, and many times he thought of the darkness he had walked in his entire life. He thought he was enlightened, and now he knew better. The darkness of his past belief system was as hopeless and black as his present blindness. A deep dredging of Saul's heart was occurring. A destruction of an old pattern of thinking, and a new way of the spirit being introduced as Saul sat in his black hopeless world. Saul never felt so shattered and helpless.

After three days, a man named Ananias came to Saul with a pronouncement. "Brother Saul, the Lord Jesus, who appeared to you on the road as you came, has sent me that you may receive your sight and be filled with the Holy Spirit." What a day for Saul. Jesus introduces Saul to real sight; to a real relationship in the spirit with Jesus; to a way of life that defers to the lead of the Holy Spirit; to a life where you rest in the Holy Spirit; to a life in the tree of life, a whole new way of thinking and living in harmony with the Lord Jesus.

There are so many parallels and much symbolism in this story of Saul leaving *organized religion and legalism*, and entering into the new way of the spirit, that I would suggest you prayerfully spend time meditating on Saul's journey. Did you notice the high level of pain he experienced mentally and emotionally as his world fell apart? Is that the way you are feeling right now? Did you notice how you can live for years very zealously worshiping God out of the tree of the knowledge of good and evil, and not even realize it? Saul did. So have many of us.

When Saul, who becomes Paul, starts to live in the tree of life he becomes a new creation and does many truly great things in the service of God. We can too. During the deep state of depression and shock Saul spiraled into, he never dreamed he would serve the Lord in such a profound way as he later did. During those three days of blindness he probably considered his life and ministry over forever. Not so with the Lord Jesus. He loves us so much; he will go to a shocking extent to save us from the tree of the knowledge of good and evil. After all the pain and purifying, we will be introduced to the tree of life and a whole new walk with Jesus. Thank God for burnout!

Saul had loved God with all his heart, yet from the tree of the knowledge of good and evil.

A whole new world of thinking and living that Saul *never knew existed* was opening for him.

Saul had never understood the tree of life. Now he would become one of the major teachers of the tree of life. He would preach grace and forgiveness in profusion just as he had received it himself.

NOTES:

NOTES:

NOTES:

Chapter 10

The Great Blessing

So, as you sit, perhaps in great internal pain and burnout, ready to walk away from the church, what would you say would be the greatest blessing you could experience in this life? Healing of mind and emotions? Getting the respect you deserve instead of attacks from enemies?

How about God blessing you with a mega-church where people simply flock because everything is so cool there? How about a board of directors for your church that loves you so much they vote to give you a $100,000 dollar raise in salary? What would you consider the greatest blessing you could be given? Healing from a fatal disease? Have all your children answer their calling and be wonderfully dedicated Christians?

How about this one? To experience and participate in the sufferings of Jesus! Alright, let's go for it, everyone shouts! Uh . . . not really. But . . . it is closer to true that ten million other choices you could make.

We are here on purpose. This is the staging ground for eternity. Everything here on planet earth has its purpose to that end. When I read my Bible I am told many things by Jesus and Paul; many things that imply or bluntly state that I will suffer, and enter the kingdom of God through MUCH tribulation. I do enjoy very much the good times and times of blessings. I wish it were that way all the time. But, if it wasn't that way for Jesus, who am I to complain when I, too, have to suffer and be humbled? Jesus learned obedience through the things which he suffered. It is part of the preparation process for eternity.

Life is set up in a fashion to work against my selfishness and show me that joy is mine when I die to my selfishness and allow the Holy Spirit to carry out our Father's will. When I want things my way, I live in the tree of the knowledge of good and evil and frustration is often the fruit of my action. When I die to self, rest in the very Spirit of Jesus, and allow the Holy Spirit to lead me into the branches of the tree of life, suddenly Christianity is no longer a religion, but a dynamic spiritual relationship with Jesus. Life on earth still doesn't work my way, but it does work God's way. Life prepares me for eternity.

The point of life on earth is to make a choice, preferably choosing life, and then learning to trust God completely even with our very lives, so when we are in eternity we will live in harmony with God forever! To that end, I must learn to completely surrender my life, and allow God's life (Jesus) to live in me. It is not an easy thing. God helps me out by allowing me to suffer for my own good. For example, God gives us children. He does not give us children so we can help them grow up. Rather, he gives us children so we will grow up! When you spend weeks at a time walking a baby with colic back and forth across the living room carpet from midnight until four AM every night, you learn what it means to lay down your life for another.

When I can't find my pen, I can put on Godly character by staying in the tree of life or I can get upset and react out of the tree of the knowledge of good and evil and make myself and everyone around me tense. When I am mistreated by people at church, I have a choice. Respond in the tree of life and put on Godliness because of that response, or, respond from the tree of the knowledge of good and evil, and make life at church difficult for everyone.

We need not debate whether the Christian walk is one of

endless joy or many sorrows and suffering. If you have lived any length of time, you know this life contains both blessings and suffering. What is more important is our response to both. Critically important is our attitude toward both blessing and suffering. When it comes to resting in the very spirit of Jesus, a blessing can become a curse, and when we truly desire righteousness, suffering that purifies can be a great blessing!

Viewpoint becomes important to enduring unto the end in the Christian walk. It is what the two trees are all about. If you are deeply wounded or burned out at the moment, you may be so disillusioned with church and Christianity you may be thinking of walking away from it all. Please read the rest of this book. The remainder is dedicated to explaining the two trees and what a blessing it is to be broken and purged like you are experiencing right now. The pain you feel is horrible, but, it truly is a blessing to participate in the sufferings of Jesus.

NOTES:

NOTES:

NOTES:

Chapter 11

Welcome to Lo Debar

Lo Debar. The name means "*no green thing*". It was a dry, brown patch of desert on the outskirts of David's kingdom. The type of town that attracted any drifting has-been, or reject of any type. It was a rough town, where the down and out and the deeply depressed could hang out with little hassle from the outside world; a town that symbolized no hope, no future.

It is in this town a man named Mephibosheth lives. He is a small time terrorist who picks away at the fringes of David's kingdom sporadically. He isn't much to look at. Both his legs are crippled and he stumbles around town on a pair of crutches he often curses. On his belt is a razor sharp dagger, and deep in his heart runs a wound deeper than any blade could cut. Mephibosheth's temperament is infamous for outbursts of anger and curses upon the king.

If he could just get one chance to thrust his dagger into King David's heart, somehow he would feel his life counted for something. Just one chance, and maybe the wound in his own heart would ease in pain. Often, in the cool of the evening, he sits out by the door to his shack, watching the evening sun dip toward the horizon, and he dreams of what it must have been like when his grandfather Saul was King of the land, and his father, Jonathan, looked forward to being the next King. If he could just avenge his father and grandfather, if he could just kill this King David who stole his throne, maybe his bitterness would subside. Little does Mephibosheth know, his chance is coming, sooner than he can imagine, but let me give you the background details.

Samuel was the man of God to the nation. The day came when the people of the nation voted God out and said they wanted a king they could see with their eyes and touch with their hands. They wanted what other nations had. A visible King they could follow. Samuel was shocked and felt rejected. God comforted him and explained that voting God out is what people do a great deal of, and that it was God they were truly rejecting, not him.

A man named Saul was made King of Israel. He looked the part. Tall, broad shouldered, and majestic looking, Saul was exactly what the people wanted. The nation could now live in the illusion it had created. Somehow, living in an illusion is appealing, probably because the people can adjust the illusion to suit the need or mood of the day. Illusion has an attraction that often overpowers reality. Having a physical king seems more real, and adds some legitimacy to your existence. At least they thought so, even if Samuel and God disagreed.

Time marched on like the soldiers in Saul's army, and a young shepherd boy named David came along and slew the giant Goliath. As relationships often are in the tree of the knowledge of good and evil, things went swimmingly between Saul and David for a time, but as relationships go in that same tree, the good doesn't last.

David became the star in the battles which came, and the crowds started singing songs of the ten thousands David had slain. These same songs contained verses that did not flatter Saul. The rift began. While Saul's life started to unwind, his son Jonathan drew closer to David.

Kindred spirits would be a good way to describe David and Jonathan. Both had a deep love for God, in a way that Saul would never understand. Jonathan was the son of Saul, yet his heart and mind were so different, so faithful and loyal to the desires of the great God. The relationship between David and Jonathan quickly deepened into something that would echo across the centuries to show us all the power of love and covenant.

As Saul's life fell apart his mind was open to demonic influence, as often is the case with those who purposely choose the tree of good and evil. He became twisted in his thinking and the idea of doing away with David became strong in his heart. Jonathan decided action was needed.

David and Jonathan entered into a blood covenant in the depths of their relationship (1 Sam. 20). As was the practice, as they made the blood covenant, they mingled their blood, and bound each other together with a love we can only describe as blood covenant love. A love that runs deeper than any human love. A love that has power in it, Godly power, as the very nature of the love itself. The two men became stronger, as the power of blood covenant love flowed back and forth between them. Their spirits were united with each other and with God in a way that is not possible outside of blood covenant.

Time went on and King Saul's mind and character twisted downward, dragging the nation reluctantly behind. Once Jonathan is convinced his father wants to kill David, Jonathan returns to David a second time and Jonathan and David expand their covenant to include all of their descendants.

Jonathan returns to David a third time, and carries out an act that is truly historic in Israel. Jonathan comes and comforts David (1 Sam. 23), and confirms to him that David will indeed be King, because God has decreed it, and that he, Jonathan, will renounce any claim to the throne. All Jonathan wants is to be a prince at David's right hand. This incredible loving act of Jonathan's sets the nation free from the curse of the throne of rebellion and paves the way for David to be King of a nation with no curse upon the people who rejected

God and wanted a human king. Jonathan is a true giant of the Old Testament, and an example of what the flow of blood covenant love can do inside a person who loves God.

David has many chances to kill King Saul, but does not. Rather, he waits for God to work out all the details. The day comes in battle with the Philistines, where Jonathan is killed and in a fit of great grief, Saul falls on his own sword. The door is open for David to take the throne God has given him.

The family of Saul hears the tragic news back in Jerusalem, and they decide to flee, fearing both David and the Philistines. In shock and panic they make a mad rush for the hills, and in the events that follow, Jonathan's baby son, Mephibosheth, is dropped by the nurse-maid as they all run at top speed. Baby Mephibosheth is crippled in both legs, but the family does manage to escape.

Over the next many years these two men, young Mephibosheth, and King David, are busy moving in opposite directions. David is establishing his kingdom and settling the region down after the war with the Philistines. Mephibosheth is growing up and being fed lies and half-truths about the king and how he stole the throne from Mephibosheth. As the years roll by, Mephibosheth's heart and mind are embittered toward the king. The pain and feelings of revenge run deep in his spirit. He develops into a small time terrorist on the fringes of David's kingdom, picking away when he can and spreading his hate for the king at every opportunity.

So, with that background, let me tell you the extraordinary events that are about to unfold! They are life-giving and life changing!

David has his kingdom well in hand. Now he asks his advisors if there are any descendants of the family of Saul still about. He is informed of Mephibosheth, and he desires to share the blood covenant love he had for Jonathan with

Mephibosheth. It is the very nature of blood covenant love. This love needs to flow. It is a river of life to those who have experienced it. David needed to give it away as much as a terrorist like Mephibosheth needed it to change his bitter heart. David hunts for Mephibosheth throughout the kingdom.

To Mephibosheth, I'm sure it appears the end of the line when he hears the many hooves of David's army horses riding into Lo Debar. He knew he would hear such a sound one day, but when it comes he is not quite ready. Mephibosheth reaches for his crutches and struggles to his feet. With an effort he makes his way to the door to meet his end at the hands of a man he hates more then anyone, the very man who stole his throne from him.

David is not among the soldiers. They inform Mephibosheth that the king wants to see him, and with head hanging, Mephibosheth is placed on a horse and taken off to Jerusalem. He enters the palace slowly in his crippled state and ponders the fact he should be the one living here. Well, at least I will die here, he thinks to himself.

King David enters the room, and after standing directly in front of Mephibosheth and eyeing him up and down, David smiles a warm, even loving grin at this crippled terrorist. Mephibosheth is bewildered at this smile, and stares at the floor feeling very uncomfortable. What is this sadistic king up to? Why is he tormenting me with such a grin just before he slays me?

"Don't be afraid," David said. Again the warm smile returns to the King's face. A smile that has a love to it Mephibosheth has never experienced before. "I will show you kindness for the sake of your father, Jonathan. You see, young man, I made a blood covenant with your father, Jonathan, before you were even conceived in your mother's womb. When you were born you became an inheritor of that love that flowed between your father and me. The peace and care we had for one another now flows toward you. We have your grandfather Saul's land and wealth, and your father Jonathan's land and wealth also saved for you. All the flocks and herds and lands, they are yours now, Mephibosheth. And, I want you to come and live here in the King's palace with me and break the bread of the covenant with me every night at my table."

Mephibosheth feels odd, strangely suspicious. His mind is racing and spinning in a hundred directions. Are my ears working properly, he thinks? This is not normal behavior for any king. Can this be? "What is your servant that you should notice a dead dog like me?" Mephibosheth whispers.

The warmth and hope that comes from blood covenant love beams across David's face. The love flows from David into Mephibosheth and starts to soften his heart. "You see, a covenant is not something a human can change, Mephibosheth," David began. "When your father and I mingled blood and covenanted with one another we made it for generations to come. The love I had for your father I now have for you. I wish this Godly love to flow through me to you and heal you of all your hurts and wounds. There is nothing you can do to earn it. You can't pay for it or qualify for it. You are part of the covenant. You are an inheritor. Let me love you, Mephibosheth! Let me love you the way I loved your father, Jonathan!"

Mephibosheth is speechless. This offer seems beyond his wildest imagination. He ponders his choices. If I say no, then I am dead because I am an enemy of the King. And, I am dead a second time over because if I say no, I am a breaker of the covenant, and that means death. If I say yes, I will be an inheritor of all my family's wealth and land, plus an inheritor of the love my father shared with this man, David. Hmmm . . .

Already the flow of covenant love is affecting Mephibosheth's heart. The hard-boiled leather skin of his spirit is starting to soften. It requires time, but the process is under way. In time he will fully enter into the opportunity, and the steady flow of blood covenant love from David everyday keeps loving away the evil and bitterness in Mephibosheth's heart. As Mephibosheth allows these changes to occur from the inside out, he starts to love King David back with blood covenant love. When this begins to happen, Mephibosheth enters into the very spirit of his father Jonathan. He enters into the very spirit of his covenant representative. It is nothing short of a miracle performed by the flow of blood covenant love!

King David has followed a new path. A new trail. A new covenant. Instead of killing his enemy, he loves him with blood covenant love. Instead of doing the tree of good and evil thing, and killing him, David does the tree of life thing, and reaches inside his enemy with blood covenant love, which changes Mephibosheth from the inside out. All the bitterness, hatred, envy, disgust, frustration and disillusionment inside of Mephibosheth is washed away with blood covenant love, and replaced with a new spirit.

Here, in this story are some of the greatest dynamics of the spirit dimension. Follow me closely, please. As the king poured life and covenant love into the spirit of Mephibosheth, this young terrorist started taking on *the very spirit of his covenant representative*! In other terms, Mephibosheth started to lose his evil hatred, and started to slowly take on the very spirit and attitude of his father, Jonathan. Mephibosheth, over time, left the realm of hating the king, and entered into the mind and heart of covenant love for the king. Mephibosheth became in a real sense a new creation, with a whole new spirit fueling him. No longer a terrorist, and now a lover and supporter of the king! And here's the deal – it all *starts* and *finishes* with the king. Mephibosheth was not making it happen, or striving for it!

Hello?

When you and I just give up, stop all the endless striving, and just let King Jesus love us, and allow that love in, our heart, mind and spirit will start to take on the very mind, heart and spirit of your covenant rep – Jesus Himself! AMEN.

Please ponder this, and come to understand how the spirits work – your human spirit, Jesus' spirit of love and the Holy Spirit. The flow of life and covenant love can reach right inside a person – past their head and heart, all the way to their spirit and create a healing.

Healing today happens the same way. Your healing! Let the King love you!

NOTES:

NOTES:

NOTES:

Chapter 12

Soup with Elisha – Religion is Poisonous

As a child did you ever suspect your mother of trying to poison you? Probably not! Why would she? She loves you, right?

Elisha is teaching at the school of prophets in Gilgal. One of the group is sent out to prepare the lunch stew, and he gathers all kinds of good stuff, including some gourds that looked great! The good fellow mixes the stew and simmers it to perfection. The hearty aroma teases all the students while Elisha teaches. Finally, lunch break arrives, and with peaking anticipation, all sit down to eat.

It all seems too good to be true. It is!

"It's poison!" someone shouts, "Death in the pot!" Elisha fixes the poisonous pot of stew and it becomes nutritious for the group. No one ever dreamed the cook would put death in the stew because he eats from the same pot! The food must be good and blessed of God! Yes?

No!

It turns out this is not the case. Kind of sounds like the modern church with its' twenty-five versions of the gospel, eh? Just because the dynamic preacher stands up and gives a loud, colorful sermon, doesn't mean the Holy Spirit inspired the message. The message might move you, perhaps the selfish side of you, but it may still be death in the pot. The preacher is eating the same spiritual diet, and he, too, will die spiritually.

Few would ever suspect their mother, or their pastor, of feeding them poison. But it can happen. Of all the poison we could eat in our spiritual diet, perhaps the most subtle and deadly is a concoction known as *religion*. Like a wild gourd that looks delicious in a stew pot, religion and all it's trappings look and smell great as it creeps into our churches.

We live in a world that lends its approach to religion. Human nature likes things *to do*. From our youth in boy and girl scouts, to 4H, to university, we love fulfilling certain tasks and then receiving the reward, a nice badge to sew on our shirt. All through adult life we have ladders to climb, with rewards given with each rung of the ladder. Even when we buy a new product, like a DVD player, it comes with an instruction booklet. We are told how to make the DVD player work; step 1, step 2, step 3. When you buy a bookcase from a discount furniture store, your bookcase comes with assembling instructions. Step 1, step 2, step 3. Try baking a cake! The step by step process is called a *recipe*. When we are following the process to create a chemical or solve a math problem, it is called a *formula*. When we are starting a machine, the step by step procedure is called the *operating instructions*, or *start up procedure*.

We become addicted to following methods, steps, keys, secrets, techniques, approaches, paths, patterns, methodologies, plans, courses, tactics, policies, curricula or programs. Some people thrive so well in this structured environment, they simply can never understand someone who can't fit into *their* box. Or, more troubling yet, what do you do when someone comes along and suggests a different box? Now we have the makings of a war!

Let's go back to the Garden of Eden and have another look. After eating from the tree of the knowledge of good and evil, the man and woman run away from God. God is now feared incorrectly by man. The people now have shame and guilt to cover up. God tries to draw out the man and woman with questions. He is gently urging the people to repent. They choose the road of victimization and self-justification instead. From that moment on, the human race has approached God with the wrong kind of fear. So, the name of the game is appeasement, impress God if you can, or manipulate God to bless you in the manner you desire.

"Great, so Mr. Pastor, just tell me what to do and I'll do it, then God will accept me, or better yet, God will bless me! Tell me the steps, the seven keys to better blessings. Give me the three secrets to helping my rebellious teen. Tell me the five techniques for developing my leadership skills. I'm unhappy. Give me three Biblical keys to happiness!"

It all seems so natural and logical to our procedure driven mind and culture. Under the Old Covenant, God gave man an entire system to live by. The Lord gave them procedures and methods to follow in formal worship, and the performing of the temple sacrifices. Every detail of life, from clothing to clean and unclean foods was clearly spelled out. They even had a series of Holy Days that gave them a calendar to follow in the development of their culture.

In all the "thou shalts" and "thou shalt nots" of the Old Testament, God gave them formulas and recipes for blessings and curses. For the procedure driven success oriented ladder climber, this must have been a dream come true. Heaven on earth as some would say!

Wrong!

It was the wisdom of God allowing mankind to see for himself, even with the perfect recipe for success with success promised by God himself, man proved he could not consistently follow the recipe! Man would inevitably fall off the ladder. Man would never reach holiness, righteousness and Godly character by following recipes. All man could achieve, despite formulas and methodologies, was death.

Have we in the New Covenant church learned the lessons of the Old Testament? Do we understand the new relationship we have with God is love and blood driven, not performance driven? Do we understand success is guaranteed by the flow of Jesus' blood, not the flow of our own striving sweat?

One of the characteristics of religion is it always has *something for us to do.* Our flesh is happy when we have something to reach for. It gives us the birth of pride. We look forward to telling others "*we did it.*" In that recipe for pride, are the seeds of discontent and burnout. If you fail many times over, you truly feel like a loser.

We can get so geared to what we should do, we define Christianity by those actions. "I used to read smutty pocket books, now, I read the Bible." "I used to hang out at the bar, now I hang out at the prayer small group." "I used to curse and swear, now I sing praises to God! So, I guess I am now a Christian!"

Suddenly, without us even realizing it, the New Covenant is shockingly similar to the Old Covenant. Here's what you can do, and here's what you shouldn't do. Suddenly a dynamic spiritual relationship with the Heavenly God, Himself, is reduced down to a cake recipe.

Religion can creep into marriage the same way. A good marriage is the connecting of three spirits, husband, wife, and Jesus the King. In this triune interfacing of spirits there is the flow of blood covenant love and God life. That's a great marriage. Go down to your local Bible book store and look at the titles of many marriage books. Promises of "keys," and "secrets," and Biblical "steps" to a great marriage are implied. In any relationship, be it God with man, husband and wife, or parent and child, we are speaking of spirits coming into communion, not just physical interaction. The commune of spirits can not be dissected into a cake recipe!

Even if the keys or steps sound good, please remember, if husband and wife are speaking death to one another, there is the flow of death in their marriage. People can be married for twenty or thirty years, then, wake up one morning and realize they no longer love each other. How can that happen? Easy. When you speak death into a connecting of spirits, one day the love is gone completely, and a wall of death separates the two spirits. They come to the conclusion they simply grew apart as the years passed, and it's time to move on. It's sad.

Recipes, formulas and steps are good when we are speaking of physical tasks in a physical world. When we get into dynamic relationships that involve the communing of spirits, we are speaking of a different dimension. No seven secret steps created by a church leader in his office is going to help on the spirit plane. What is needed is the flow of covenant love and God life.

Can we state clearly what the New Covenant walk is for the believer? God first loved us. The greatest example of that is the sacrifice of His son for our eternal futures. That redeeming action on the cross broke down the wall of sin and death between God's spirit and our spirit. Now, His covenant love and life can flow from His spirit to ours. This process allows the Holy Spirit to create in us a new mind and heart and a totally healed human spirit. When our spirit is in communion with God's, we start to love Him because He first loved us – hey, I think I read that in an important book somewhere!

New Covenant Christianity is all about our spirits communing with God's spirit, with the back and forth flow of blood covenant love and God life. (No wonder believers are to worship Him in spirit and in truth!)

But the flesh cries out for a physical expression. The flesh wants to bring God and worship down to a physical tangible level. So what does the flesh do under the New Covenant? It creates its own actions and rituals that have meaning to the Christian walk. For example, the "altar call". Charles Finney got this practice started approximately 155 years ago. While he was preaching he would invite people who were moved by the gospel to come forward and sit in the front pew. After the service was over, Finney and other pastors would then chat with the people sitting in the front row and counsel them to a commitment if they were ready. Since then the altar call has become a tool that some have used to a level of abuse. The altar call is a man made tool, and in the wrong hands, it can be anything from mild manipulation, to a total sham that turns off the lost world completely. In some churches this die-hard approach to the altar call has convinced the congregation that nothing good can happen unless you come forward and kneel at the altar. Some people have made over a hundred trips up to the altar and don't feel any closer to God now than they did after the first trip. Is there more Holy Spirit up there at the stage? If so, the most unconverted person in the church must be the sound man, because his sound control booth is usually at the back of the sanctuary! Poor guy!

Remember the Samaritan woman at the well in John chapter 4? In verse 20 she mentions the fact that the Jews think you must worship God in Jerusalem, after all, that's where the altar is!

Listen to the answer Jesus gives. "Woman, believe me, the hour is coming when you will neither on this mountain nor in Jerusalem, worship the Father. . . . but the hour is coming, and now is, when the true worshipers will worship the Father in spirit and truth; for the Father is seeking such to worship Him.' (John 4:21, 23 NKJV)

Interesting! According to Jesus, location is not the issue anymore. Now worship is a spiritual activity. So, the believers sitting on the 39th row of chairs are just as close to the Holy Spirit as those who kneel at the foot of the stage! You see, the Holy Spirit lives *inside of us*.

"Yes, but, the flow of God's spirit can be more powerful at the altar!"

Yes and no. Again, I would argue strongly that location *is not* the determining factor, but rather the *heart* of the believer is the issue. A manipulated person who comes down to the alter because the pastor has played games with his emotions during the altar call may not feel any flow of the spirit. Back on row 39, the totally broken believers in the right state of heart may have a flow of love, life and spirit pouring through them like Niagara Falls.

Why am I making an issue out of this? Simple. Religion, and the "things" it has us do can set you up for deep disillusionment and burnout. Some people feel a strong presence of God when they come to the altar in church. Some make a hundred trips to the altar and feel nothing. That person may feel robbed, or totally inadequate. Both may be firm believers in God's eyes. A device of man has given one person a problem that leaves them questioning their faith.

Religion is a tool of the enemy designed to place you at odds with God. "Father, I did everything I was supposed to do, and it didn't work. Why don't you love me, God?"

When it comes to giving birth in the spirit, I am one to say, leave that up to the Holy Spirit. He knows the best timing for each person. We would never approach a lady who is six months pregnant, and say in a manipulating manner, "Hey, come on now, quit sitting on the fence and give birth to that baby. Let's get that baby born now! Here, drink a gallon of castor oil and let's get those contractions started!"

The very idea is ludicrous! No, when it comes to physical birth, we know the value of having a baby go full term. Why do some preachers not know that when it comes to spiritual birth? What happens when spiritual birth is forced through manipulation? I would say there is a good chance of premature death. Better to leave the Holy Spirit to bring the lost along at the best pace for each person, and simply let us speak life and love into the spirit of the lost every chance we get.

Wrong use of altar calls is simply one example of religion in the modern church. Beware of any device invented by man. Beware of promises that seem too good to be true. Read your Bible and be well educated in the Word. Don't allow yourself to be set up for disappointment and disillusionment. Those are contributing factors in burnout.

New Covenant Christianity is a communing of spirits with the flow of blood covenant love and God life between the spirits, freeing the Holy Spirit to create a new mind and heart within us. As that new mind and heart mature, *fruits* of the Holy Spirit manifest, like love, joy, peace, patience, kindness, gentleness, meekness and faith. Also, wonderful *by-products* emerge like having the desire to read the Bible, pray, hang out with the prayer small group, and sing praise to God.

Did you catch that? Behavior change is a *by-product* of Christianity. Any time we legislate behavior through religion, the flesh resists. When behavior change comes through the new mind and heart created by the Holy Spirit, the behavior change is natural and welcome.

Let's use the motor boat example. If we have a motor boat traveling south because the auto pilot is set for south, we can bring about a direction change with outside physical means called pressure. You grab the steering wheel and force the boat to head north. Internally, the auto pilot is still set to south, so you must keep constant pressure on the steering wheel to keep the boat going north. How would you like to do this for eternity? I don't think so. After a time, the constant pressure on your arms gets really old, dude! Better to reach *inside* and reset the auto pilot of the boat to north, so that direction becomes natural! And that, my friend, is exactly what the Holy Spirit is doing inside us in the New Covenant we have with our heavenly Father!

Christianity is not a behavior modification program. Religion is often a behavior program with empty promises attached to certain behaviors that leave people disillusioned.

Religion is a tool of the Devil to separate us from God. Here are some basic characteristics of religion:

-preaching sounds very religious

-religion often is hyper sensitive to right and wrong

-religion always has something for us to do, to perform

-religion loves recipes, keys, secrets, steps, rituals, programs, manuals

-religion often contains exaggerated promises

-religion has to do with pleasing God (appeasing)

-religion has to do with living up to certain behaviors

-religion places God in a box and states God only does things this way

-religion draws circles and demands you live within the circle

-religion hates the simplicity of Christ

-religion hates the completely free expression of God's grace

-religion hates the completely free flow of God's love

-religion hates the fact God is doing the New Covenant Himself

-religion finds fault with other's prayers or worship

NOTES:

NOTES:

NOTES:

Chapter 13

Can I Have Hope Again?

Spiritual burnout is a humbling experience. You are not only worn out physically, mentally and emotionally, you also have lost much of your hope and your ideals. You are well past over-engagement and over-reactive emotions, and now your blunted emotions are taking you further into disengagement.

You are now demoralized, depressed, and disillusioned. You might even be angry with God. In your growing state of helplessness and hopelessness you may have questions like these: "Will I ever have hope again?" "Will I ever trust God again as much as before?" "Am I ever going to get my zeal back?" "I don't even feel like going to church. Will that change in time?"

At Smoldering Wick Ministries we want to befriend you and help you in the direction of healing. One of the best ways we know to do just that, is to disciple you in "Tree of Life" living and ministry. By helping you plunge into the Tree of Life we will be helping place you in a position where the Holy Spirit can do His deep inner healing. Whether you ever return to the ministry will ultimately be your decision, but with healing from burnout and a sound life-giving approach to life and ministry, the desire to return to your calling may become strong again.

After you start healing, your zeal will be tempered by your wisdom and experience. No longer will youthful idealism that is exaggerated set you up for disappointment. No longer will insecurity haunt you as a ministry leader. No longer will you take people's freedom away and try to make them over in your own image. No longer will you try to solve everyone's problems yourself. No longer will you be driven to frustration by hard-to-get-along-with people.

We desire to love God with our whole hearts. Some of us, however, have loved and served God with an incorrect approach that has hurt us and our followers. If we are left disillusioned by our experience in the ministry, it is because *we first believed in an illusion*!

Kathy and I slaved away for twenty years, ministering in a legalistic denomination where the underlying operating system was fear and control. God in His infinite wisdom brought three people into our lives that changed our whole approach to life and ministry. Malcolm Smith, headquartered in San Antonio, Texas, taught us the fallacy of legalism and religion, and introduced us to Father's unconditional love in a way we had never understood it before.

While this mind and heart opening process with Malcolm was occurring, we met Ted Haggard for the first time. What impacted us powerfully was Pastor Ted's way of thinking. It was about as far from our legalistic denomination as you could get. He was filled with love and encouragement. His views were optimistic, and truly life-giving. We were learning a whole new way of thinking!

After moving to Colorado, we were introduced to Dr. Larry Crabb. All the pieces fell together and great inner healing continued in our spirits. This book is a compilation of what we learned through our burnout after 23 years in the ministry, and what we learned through the healing process. We hope, with Father's grace and blessing that this information will help you heal and, further, help prepare you for a ministry with the Tree of Life as the *modus operandi.*

We will begin part two of this book by looking at what we have been digesting in our spiritual diet. Then we will look at the Tree of the Knowledge of Good and Evil, and see how this tree can mislead even the most sincere ministry leader. What happens when we are operating out of the Tree of the Knowledge of Good and Evil?

Then we will take a close look at what the Tree of Life is all about, and what an incredible difference in *thinking* and *living* this tree makes in our lives. We hope you will read and study this book several times and plunge yourself into the Tree of Life in your personal life, family life, and your future ministry as God reveals what that will be. Yes, you can have hope again! A more accurate, unshakable hope based on an accurate Gospel. God bless you, and please do use your burnout as a launch pad into a brighter, properly fulfilling future.

NOTES:

NOTES:

NOTES:

Chapter 14

Two Trees, Two Directions

Adam and Eve walked in the garden with God in innocence. Everything they experienced was positive. The conversations were up-lifting and educational. They shared laughter freely with God. The man and the woman enjoyed the greatest blessing possible – a face to face relationship with God, and all the joy that came with the experience. No one accused the other. No one mocked the other. They were not afraid of each other or their creator. They knew they had bare skin, but didn't know they were naked. They didn't make issues out of things that were never issues before. They trusted God, and never doubted His word. Why would they? He's Father. He knows what He's talking about. Their faith was simple, their attitudes pure. No one challenged them. No one doubted them. No one judged or criticized them. Everyone's attitude seemed positive and optimistic. This was a great life, and included that close loving relationship with God.

Now enters the Serpent into the Garden. The snake asks an interesting question. The very question itself introduces the woman to *a new thought* she had never pondered before. For the first time a challenge to God's credibility washes across the woman's mind. The unthinkable has been thought. Just the thought itself has changed the woman. She will never again be quite the same. She will never again be quite as innocent as she had been. Never again quite as trusting as she had been. Innocence has been tarnished.

"Mankind, can you really count on God to always have your best interests in mind? If so, why is He saying you can't know all things including the difference between Good and

Evil? If so, why does He not want you thinking in different patterns than the one He has given you, and what's so wrong with you clearly seeing evil and wrong in other people? What is God keeping from you? Why is He keeping it from you? Will you really die if you start to think differently?"

Even the concept of challenging the status quo was a new manner of thought for the woman. She had never heard anyone bring up such questions before. This new thinking was eye opening and somehow empowering to the woman. The incipient hints of independence began to fragrance the mind in an invisible way. The first undetectable aroma of self-will touched her heart. The first seeds of hell were being planted in her spirit even before she ate from the Tree of the Knowledge of Good and Evil.

Of all the trees in the garden, perhaps hundreds and hundreds of them, the man and woman could freely eat. God had explained to them not to eat from just a single tree in the center of the garden. It was a showcase tree. It could stand tall and beautiful, and showcase mankind's obedience and complete trust in God's integrity. Or, it could stand and showcase man's willingness to believe a lie, and question God's integrity.

After this challenge of God's integrity toward mankind, Adam and Eve eat from the Tree of the Knowledge of Good and Evil. Their eyes are opened; opened to a whole new way of seeing; opened to a whole new *world view;* opened to a *new value system.*

First, they notice each other's nudity. They had always been naked and it was never an issue. Now it is. They embarrass each other, for the first time. They feel shame in their hearts for the first time. Instead of working together as they always had, they now separate and cover themselves with fig leaves before coming back together again. The tree of the knowledge of good and evil now becomes *a new way to live,* not just think. Covering up their shame now becomes a daily part of life. The great cover up of anything embarrassing is now a normal response, instead of the simple innocence that was once between the man and woman. Separation and embarrassment become a part of relationships now.

Yet, not just separation on the human level, but also in human-God relationships!

Now the man and woman's best friend, God, returns. Fear now enters the human race, and the man and woman run and hide. They move away from God with this new way of thinking – this new way of seeing, this new value system. They had disobeyed their best friend and parent. Guilt enters the human race. Fear and guilt in the human heart lead to a new action. The man and woman now run away from God instead of running toward Him.

Fear, embarrassment, shame, judging and evaluating each other, covering up, and running away from your best friend – not exactly impressive fruit from this new way of thinking is it? Whatever happened to that simple innocence in the Garden that was so fulfilling and fun? Whatever happened to that child-like lifestyle where strategy and coping methods need not be invented in order to survive emotionally? Whatever happened to that peace and joy they once experienced, free from fear, shame and guilt?

Adam and Eve's best friend offers them a pathway back into walking with Him in the garden. The route is called confession and repentance. With the new way of thinking learned in the tree of the knowledge of good and evil, Adam and Eve choose the road of self-justification and victimization. Adam is so quick to point his finger at Eve and play the role of victim himself. Under the influence of the tree of the knowledge of good and evil, Eve is quick to point her finger at the serpent, and claim the role of victim for herself. Everybody is an innocent victim and somebody else is to blame. *Blame?* That's a word never heard in the Garden until the eating of the tree of the knowledge of good and evil!

"God, the woman you made is to blame for my guilt."

"God, the serpent you allowed in the Garden is to blame for my guilt."

Now we have a new value system and world-view. The world view is through the eyes of a victim. Everyone else is to blame. The value system allows the people to *know, judge*, and *blame*. The victimization and the judging and condemning of others causes even more division in relationships.

So there you have it. With this new enlightened way of thinking, God gets blamed because He put the tree of the knowledge of good and evil in the Garden to start with, and He allowed the serpent free time with the humans. Yes, sir, it's all His fault! If He really were a God of Love this would never have happened! If He were a responsible God the serpent would never have been allowed into the Garden. If God were on the ball He would not have been absent and shown up late on the scene. Yes, this tree of the knowledge of good and evil thinking is amazing, isn't it? You can so clearly see in 20/20 vision everybody's fault in the entire known world. In fact you can even see into the spirit dimension and see all of God's mistakes too! It is amazing stuff, this fruit from the tree of the knowledge of good and evil.

What is really amazing is how the world buys into this way of thinking, and sometimes ministry leaders buy in as well. Yes, even entire congregations get caught up in this manner of thinking. In Genesis chapter 3, God tells us definitively that the tree of the knowledge of good and evil *leads to death.* Even the *good* in the tree of the knowledge of good and evil leads to *death.* Stop and consider that for a moment. It's not just the evil that leads to death. It's not just sin that leads to death. Even the *good* in the tree of the knowledge of good and evil leads to death, regardless of how correct it sounds and looks. So many people in the church seem to totally forget this fact. You can sense it though, especially if you live in the tree of life. You can sit among a whole congregation and feel or sense the spirit of death in the room.

But do we believe it? When you find the basic characteristics of the tree of the knowledge of good and evil manifesting in your life – fear, greed, control, judging others, displaced responsibility, victimization, do you consider the fact it leads to death? Do we really? Sure, big time sin leads to death, but do we really believe pointing our finger at our mate and blaming them because we are late to the meeting – that action and attitude leads toward death? It does! Anytime we get into *victimization*, the thoughts and actions lead to death.

"If it weren't for my parents, I would be a normal person."

"If my mate just had the brains to understand, we would get along."

"If we had a decent senior pastor this church would double in size."

Anytime we get into that type of thinking, judging, condemning, we are taking a step toward death. Beware of members who huddle after services discussing the pastor and his approach. What are they saying? Why are they saying it? Are they really any different than the huddle of two humans and a serpent in the garden? Will the fruit be any different?

When the board of directors of the church finish the meeting and start to leave, they stand in a huddle out in the church parking lot, talking in the dark. What are they saying? Why couldn't they say it in the meeting with the pastor present?

What if you are right in what you are speaking? Sorry, that matters not. You may be 100% right. Perhaps that deacon is a gossip and a liar. In the Tree of Life you would speak words of life into that deacon, and bless him. You would love him back into life and befriend him. If you get caught up in pointing the finger and judging – even if what you say is right – it is what we call empty victory. You're right! Congratulations! Have a great time in hell, because that is where the tree of the knowledge of good and evil will take you.

By now several examples in your own experience have come to mind. You can recall deacon's meetings, or elder meetings where the spirit of judgment filled the air and nobody left feeling edified. I have spoken in legalistic judgmental churches where the spirit of death was so thick it felt like a Canadian snowstorm. Perhaps a person or two comes to mind that has a spirit you can't stand being around. They are negative, critical, and seem to have a dark doomsday cloud hanging over them. Nothing anyone else does is right. This person has built a permanent residence in the branches of the tree of the knowledge of good and evil.

Think of those people you have served that were always making issues out of matters no one really cared about. Remember how they gathered their troops and supporters around them? How they kept building the issues up in the minds of anyone who would listen, and finally you had to take the time and gut-wrenching stressful effort to try and deal with an issue that had next to nothing to do with promoting the Kingdom of God? Remember that? I thought you would. When the spirit of death starts ruling a church the leadership usually doesn't forget such "fun-filled-times."(do I sound a little sarcastic? Maybe I need to swing back into the Tree of Life before I write any more of this book!).

Quick summary of fruit from the tree of the knowledge of good and evil: fear, shame, guilt, judging others, blame, running away, displacement of responsibility, finger pointing, covering up, victimization, anger with God and fellow man.

Before taking a deeper look under the bark of the Tree of the Knowledge of Good and Evil, give yourself a good self-examination and see how much you are swinging in the branches of the tree of the knowledge of good and evil.

When you do an exam of your deep inner heart, how much damage has been done to your hope and ideals?

Honestly, have you been angry at God and taken it out on others, like mate and brethren?

If you have been *dis*illusioned in your burnout experience, do you now recognize the illusions that became part of your belief system?

Have you ever challenged God's integrity toward you by being insulted that He allowed this pain in your life?

In your ministry and personal life have you been tempted to "cover-up" something or many things?

How well have you given others their freedom?

Do you notice control tendencies in your leadership style?

Have you ever been told you were a control freak?

Do you practice giving people their freedom to such a great degree that you would leave people alone in the Garden with the Serpent? God did!

How much has fear and guilt played a role in relationships within your ministry?

In your burnout have you answered Father's call to come out of hiding, confess and repent of any wrong doing on your part regardless of other's sins and mistakes?

Are you running away from God right now?

Be honest and ask yourself, how easily do I point the finger and slip into victimization?

Are you still playing the victim now? Are you sure? What would your mate and children say?

Do you still have a deep need to tell your side of the story in the great conflict that brought on your pain?

Have you ever rallied your troops and supporters around you in a church conflict to oppose the "other side?"

Looking back over your ministry, can you remember times when life flowed through the congregation and how wonderful that was? Can you recall times when death flowed, and how hopeless it all seemed? List some of the differences between these two seasons in your ministry.

NOTES:

NOTES:

NOTES:

Chapter 15

Tree of the Knowledge of Good and Evil Under the Bark

*"Don't love the world's ways. Don't love the world's goods. Love of the world squeezes out love of the Father. Practically everything that goes on in the world – wanting your own way (fear and selfishness), wanting everything for yourself (greed), wanting to appear important (pride)- **has nothing to do with the Father**. It just isolates you from him. The world and its wanting, wanting, wanting is on the way out – but who ever does what God wants is set for eternity."* (1 John 2:15-17 The Message (emphases ours).

Let's have a good look at Genesis chapter 3 again and see how the roots of the tree of the knowledge of good and evil branch out in the limbs of the tree and bear fruit that is definitely not good. The serpent questioned God's character and integrity by making Adam and Eve wonder *if* God had their best interests at heart. Pride and greed were stirred in the people.

The root of *pride,* hidden under the dirt where eyes can't see, branches out into a limb that becomes visible to all. We can call the tree limb *control*, an obvious expression of pride. The serpent was offering what sounded like a better level of control. Now the people could see and know good and evil for themselves. They now could decide for themselves what was right and wrong. They now could determine success and failure. They now had a new value system, not coming from God. They now had a new world view, not coming from God.

Tree of Knowledge of Good and Evil – Under the Bark

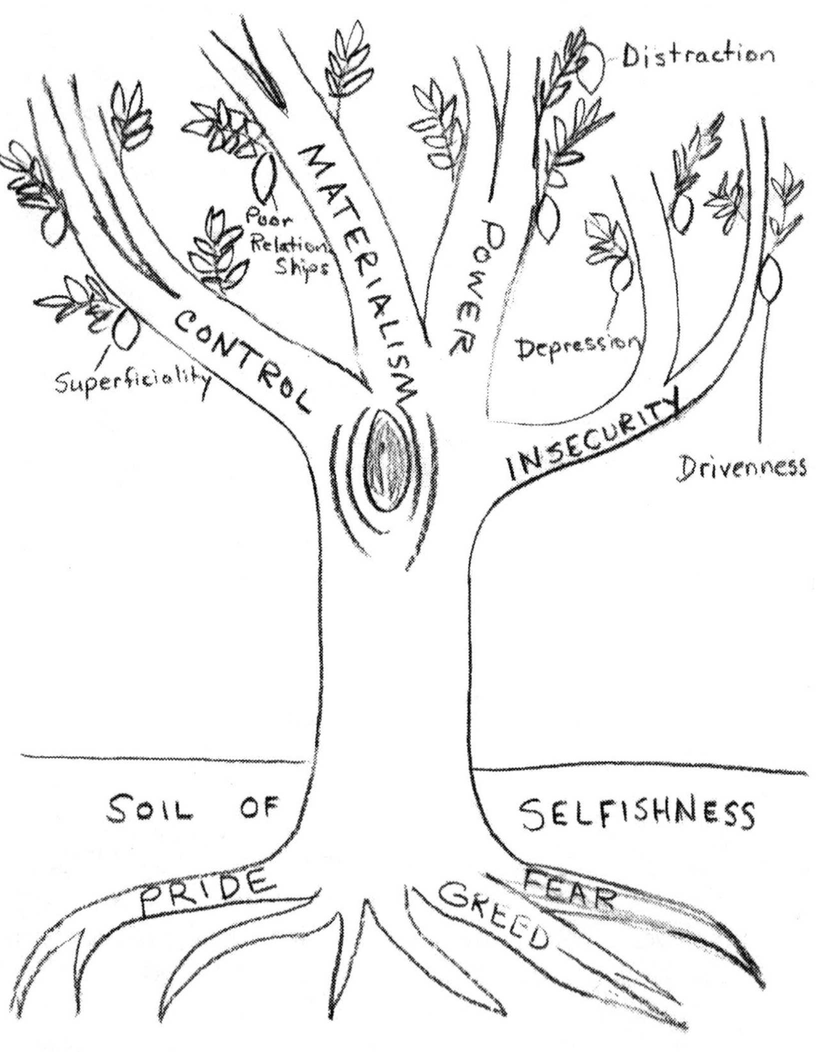

Once this limb of control has developed, what is the fruit it produces? We could call it *superficiality*. Mankind convinces himself he is really in control of his life and has his act together. He is no longer totally dependant upon God. He has become his own god. This results in mankind wearing masks in addition to fig leaves to keep up the facade of success. So, if you have the most dynamic worship band in town, you must be a great worship leader, or even senior pastor. If you had more baptisms at your church last year than any other church in town, you must be a successful leader who's got it together! If your youth group appears to be well organized and disciplined you must be the best youth pastor in the state – even if you have to use strong threats to keep them in line! So what if they call you Saddam Hussein behind your back – as long as it all looks good in public!

Modern man finds this fruit of *superficiality* manifested in ten thousand activities that define success – while their relationships with spouse, children, God, and brethren suffer and die. A Tree of Life leader understands Christianity is a relationship, not a religion, and relationships take first place over "busy-ness." A Tree of Life leader understands the life flow of God is through dynamic relationships, ***not*** religious activities.

Have you ever been eyeball to eyeball in an important conversation, two human spirits interacting with the flow of the Holy Spirit present – and the other person's cell phone rings? Suddenly, the live one-on-one conversation is dropped like a hot potato, and the unknown invisible caller on the other end of the call is given first priority.

"Hello, uh, no, no, I don't want to buy a year's supply of cat food. No, no, thanks anyway. Goodbye." "Oh, I guess we need to go now." The heart deep conversation is forgotten. No real change will come.

The tree of the knowledge of good and evil has long-reaching vines into every area of life. Destroyed relationships are the common by-product fruit.

Greed is another long dirt-covered root of the tree of the knowledge of good and evil. The serpent appealed to Adam and Eve's desire to be more like God. The desire turned evil, and became greed. The desire to be like God overwhelmed the desire to obey God. For modern man, greed often manifests in *materialism*, or perceived power and influence over others. This branch or limb of materialism or influence produces a fruit we can call *distraction*. Adam and Eve were distracted to the point of disobedience. How often are we so preoccupied with tasks and obtaining and achieving we are distracted from a deep relationship with the Lord Jesus? Again, we see the contrast between the two trees. A Tree of Life leader will focus on knowing and relating to Jesus more everyday, understanding God's life flow is through that relationship.

How many pastors and ministry leaders have I met in the past thirty years who have had so many goals and visions they ended up missing out all together on a wonderful rest with Jesus and in Jesus? Far too many. There are the pastors who read every church growth book ever printed, and still the church doesn't grow – but in the meantime the pastor's children have grown up and moved out and he doesn't know it yet! How many believers spend half their life and most of their money racing from conference to conference to hear the latest greatest speaker, hoping somehow "it" will all come together and their Christianity will work for them? For some, the endless conferences are like the "addiction kick" you get when you attend your monthly multi-level marketing meeting on your way to riches, fame and fortune – or great heartache.

Distraction is often the opposite of focus. Don't be the ministry leader who is going to save the whole world. Focus on your gifting and become a pillar in that area. Become the expert in a small area, and leave plenty of time for Jesus – after all he is the center of the plan – not you.

Fear is another major root in the tree of the knowledge of good and evil. The visible limb is called *insecurity*. It causes us to run away fast like Adam and Eve. The fruit is called, *driven*. We want to feel secure. We don't like failure. We want everyone to believe in us. We drive ourselves, and sometimes we even drive others to the breaking point. Fear causes us to hide, hide from God, or mate or reality.

Drivenness is not the classic Type A personality that is so admired and worshiped here in America. As a Canadian living in America I am always amazed how the very roots of American culture going all the way back to 1776, are incorporated into American Christianity. Success in life, business and sports are all part of the American version of the Gospel. I have always been amazed how many of the apostles and early church fathers would have been labeled total failures by the expectations that are preached in many pulpits today.

Drivenness can disguise itself as godly commitment, dedication, sacrifice for the Lord, and a dozen other terms. Jerome Daly says it well in his excellent book, Soul Space, ***"Drivenness is not a quality of the Kingdom of God. Passion is, perseverance is, determination is, but drivenness is not! If you regularly feel pressured, stressed, and always behind, then you probably struggle with drivenness."***

It is much better to simply rest (Matt 11:28) in the very spirit of Jesus.

So, what do these roots of the tree of the knowledge of good and evil look like – *fear, pride* and *greed* – in a ministry leader? A ministry leader who lives and operates in the tree of the knowledge of good and evil will have a lot of secrets and insecurities. It will be very important that the ministry look good on the outside, and a level of legalism (control) will be incorporated to insure this. Fear religion will creep in and signs of control and more control will grow. A negative dark spirit (attitude) may become very evident, and the sermons, or teachings will have a corrective tone to them far more often than inspiration or encouragement. The unconditional love of Father will not be talked about much if at all, and God may be presented more in judgment language than in love language.

People will not be given their freedom, and the only way things should be done is the way the ministry leader would do them. This expresses itself in constant evaluation of people and actions and the giving of unsolicited advice too quickly and too frequently. Freedom and creativity are stifled in the group, and love is not the most obvious quality followers notice in the ministry leader. God forbid you should ever have a different interpretation of scripture then the ministry leader in the tree of the knowledge of good and evil.

Did or do you desire more control in your ministry?

Did you wear a mask, or were you who you truly are?

How big is your carnal ego? How important was it for everything to look right on the outside?

Honestly, how much do you worry about what people think?

Are you more relationship oriented, or task oriented? Are you sure? Does it bother you when tasks are not done and therefore things look disorganized?

How much does it bother you when tasks are not completed? Does your wrath sometimes spill out on the brethren or your own family?

Would others describe you as a relationship oriented leader with sharp focus, or a person of endless goals and dreams?

Have you started building your "pillar" in the church so many times in so many different avenues that you look back on your ministry and what you see are a dozen pillars of various heights, but none of them reach the roof?

Can you clearly see the difference between passion and drivenness?

Do you have secrets and insecurities?

NOTES:

NOTES:

NOTES:

Chapter 16

Tree of Life – Walking in Innocence and Freedom

Stop and think about the neutral ground in the Garden of Eden prior to Adam and Eve eating from the tree of the knowledge of good and evil. They had not eaten from the tree of life, but death was not yet flowing in their lives or relationships either. So, they enjoyed a close loving friendship with God, and each other. No judging of one another. No criticism of each other. No evaluating and laughing at each other. No finger pointing. No negative attitudes. No secrets. No lies. No insecurities. Even without eating from the Tree of Life it sounds better than the last church you served in, doesn't it?

Now, what if we add the Tree of Life into the equation? What might be possible? How wonderful could life and ministry and church actually be if everyone was away from the tree of the knowledge of good and evil, and eating from the tree of life?

Let's explore the tree of life a little more and understand the root system, the limbs and the fruit they produce.

"*And now these three remain: faith, hope and love. But the greatest of these is love*."

1Corinthians13:13 NIV.

"*God is love. Whoever lives in love, lives in God, and God in him.*" 1 John 4:16b NIV.

The Tree of Life – Under the Bark

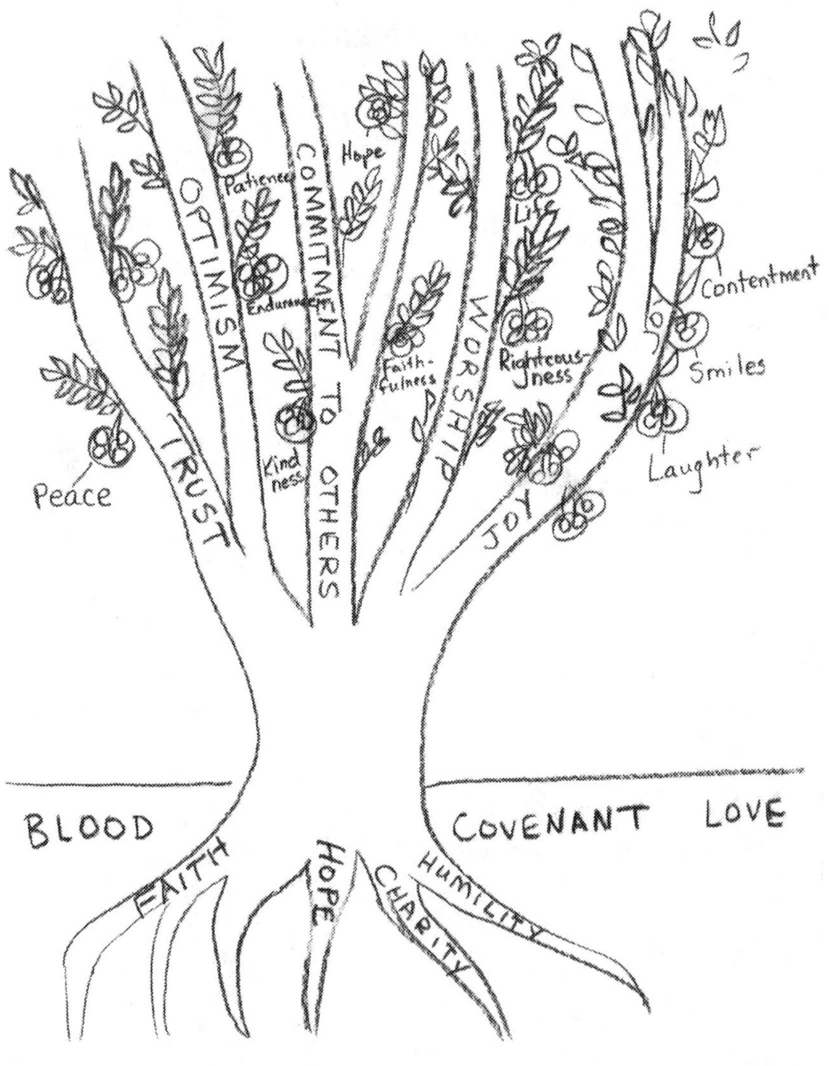

To have a deep tap root called *love* is a wonderful thing. Love is outgoing toward another's good. When love flows from us like a mighty river, it impacts others in the best way possible. We could call the manifesting limb *service* to others. In time, as the flow of love leaving us to serve others creates a wonderful fruit that surpasses happiness. It is a fruit called *joy*.

The term happy comes from the old English word hap. A hap has to do with luck. Often these events are beyond our control. When our luck is good and several haps occur that we are hoping for, we say we are *happy*. When one or more haps come our way that we did not want to occur, we are *un*-happy.

The joy of living in the tree of life *is not* a result of luck or circumstance, but a solid fruit growing on the limb of service to others, being fed and developed by the root of love. This is the essence of the Two Great Commandments.

Faith as a root produces a limb called *trust.* When this limb called trust in God produces its wonderful fruit, we call it *peace*. When you live in the tree of life, Father watches out for you. You need not worry like those who don't know God. You don't fuss and fume about what you don't have. You relax and rest in the Lord, and have peace of mind. It's His plan, His church, His ministry, His problems, His problem people, His challenges, He is the center of the plan, not us. We can relax and have peace. Amen!

Hope. With hope as a root in the tree of life, the heart is not made sick. Instead the limb of *optimism* produces fruits like *patience, endurance* and *faithfulness*. People living in life smile more and see the future with a positive slant. The tree of the knowledge of good and evil person is so busy with his conspiracy theories and figuring out who did what wrong that they have little time for smiling and loving others.

Humility is certainly another root in the tree of life. Have you ever met a Christian with no humility? Sure you have. It's almost enough to turn you off church all together! Jesus exemplified humility, and taught this virtue. When we truly are humble, we no longer worship ourselves in a hundred different ways, but rather, we worship God with our whole being. Humility realizes God is the center of the plan, not self, and the provider of all things. This focus branches out in a limb called *worship*, and produces a fruit called *righteousness*. To focus on God and appreciate and love Him with our whole heart results in a lifestyle and actions God likes, and calls righteous.

Living in the tree of life exemplifies the Kingdom of God as clearly stated in Romans 14:17. "*For the Kingdom of God is not a matter of eating and drinking, but of righteousness, peace, and joy in the Holy Spirit.*" NIV

If you live in the tree of the knowledge of good and evil, eating and drinking are important. After all, it involves right and wrong, good and evil. You could be sinning by eating too many chips, or drinking too many sodas! "God forbid, we better make some rules governing this action so our church will set the right example to the world! From now on any member in good standing can't drink more than two sodas a day, and can eat only one small bag of chips!" Welcome to a church filled with death, little freedom, and unhappy people.

Can you see the difference in focus between the thinking in each tree? When you live in the tree of the knowledge of good and evil you *see* in a manner that allows for knowing, judging and blaming. You can see good and evil, right and wrong so clearly. The good and evil become over-focused so easily. Churches become legalistic without even knowing it. Christianity becomes a series of actions. You no longer hang out at the bar, now you hang out at the prayer meeting. You no longer read trashy novels, now you read the Bible. You no longer curse and swear, now you sing praises to God. The big problem is – *that's not Christianity*! The three things I mentioned, prayer, Bible study and singing praises are all *by-products* of Christianity. Christianity is a deep, loving, dynamic relationship with Jesus. All that we do after we fall head over heels in love with Him, is a by-product.

So, the tree-of-the-knowledge-of-good-and-evil Christian is consumed with right and wrong, good and evil, and the outward show of holiness. By contrast, the tree of life believer is focused on life. That's it! Life! Sure, they are still aware of right and wrong, good and evil, but that is not the focus of their walk with Jesus. The tree of life believer is consumed with life and the promotion of life; speaking life, living life, thinking life, walking in life, all day every day. When a tree-of-lifer sees a brother stumble, he or she never thinks of judging or blaming, but rather asks a question. "Lord Jesus, how can I speak life into my brother, and get him moving back in the direction of life? Lord Jesus help me speak into my brother's spirit, and love him into life."

NOTES:

NOTES:

NOTES:

Chapter 17

Tree of Life – Choosing Life

As we travel through life as a ministry leader or lay-member, we make choices. The choices we make move us in a direction, either toward death or toward life. We move toward God or toward the world and the world's operating system – which leads to death.

When a ministry leader slides toward the world's operating system and still hopes for Tree of Life results in his/her ministry, disappointment and disillusionment are inevitable. The tree of the knowledge of good and evil approach to ministry has wonderful promises, with all its formulas, clichés, and programs. In view of all this exciting sophistication, the simple innocence of the tree of life seems so *naive*.

Please remember, Christianity is a relationship between bride (church) and groom (Lord Jesus) and *it is not a religion.* If you have an old version of the dictionary, look up the usage of the word *religion* from a generation ago. The word's Latin root means, "a return to bondage." Bondage or slavery wears you out. Even in my lifetime I can remember people using the word in the usage of bondage. If someone were arising every morning at four AM to train for a marathon regardless of weather conditions or personal fatigue, people would say, "John is training religiously for the Boston Marathon." In other words, John has placed himself into a self-imposed form of bondage for the sake of whipping his body into shape.

As a ministry leader you end up exhausted and totally

depleted of your own resources, because that's the energy source you are relying on. All the formulas, rituals and techniques you are using are getting very mixed results in your ministry. You're trying harder each week or month to make church life work, and your frustration with people and God is growing. You have entered into self-imposed bondage like an athlete training for a marathon, and you are growing weary.

In scripture we see Jesus sitting down and viewing the crowds. He weeps because they wander like sheep without a shepherd. Their weariness is so obvious to Jesus. They are caught in religion, and it is taking the people to death, step by step, with all the teaching about right and wrong, good and evil. The crowds are worn out, and still so far from God they don't recognize him when he walks up to them and says hello. The tree of the knowledge of good and evil seems sensible to so many people that many a ministry leader becomes seduced by its fruits.

The tree of life is not about right and wrong, good and evil. The tree of life is about life. If you choose to become *an expert* in right and wrong, good and evil, you are moving toward death. The religious leaders of Jesus' day were experts in this area. They could spot a sinner from a mile (how many cubits is that?) away. Even when they were technically correct, death surrounded them and infected everyone they came into contact with.

Jesus, however, walked in life. Life was so appealing to the sinners, they often invited Jesus over for a meal and fellowship. The sinners never felt evaluated, judged, or condemned by Jesus. They loved his presence, and the hope and respect he gave to them. It was fun to be around Life. It was invigorating for these people. *Life made them feel very different than religion.* Life filled them with joy and hope. The religion of the scribes and Pharisees made the lost feel hopelessly condemned to failure.

People who live in the tree of the knowledge of good and evil often have a presentation problem. In other words, when they see a woman who is a prostitute, they see a fallen failure. A sinner! If you walk in the tree of life like Jesus, you see a woman who is a child of God. She may be lost at the moment, but she is one of His, and needs love and respect. Jesus never called anyone a sinner. He referred to them as lost. When something valuable is lost, you spend time finding it. It is something precious, not something scorned. Jesus much preferred hanging out with the prostitutes, tax collectors, thieves, lepers, and street people – than the religious. Religious people are rarely fun to be around. To Jesus, breathing life into the lost was so much easier than breathing life into the religious! You can not eat the fruit from the tree of life when you live in the branches of the tree of the knowledge of good and evil.

God set before his people life and death, and recommended to them to choose life. Life is Jesus. He makes that clear to us in no uncertain terms. But you might say, "Yes, but we all choose Jesus." I may sound radical, but, I agree we all give Jesus lip service. Many choose religion after a short time and get caught up in doing religious activities. Religion always has something for us to do! Religion is all about pleasing and impressing God so he will bless us. Religion wears you out and disillusions you. No, I'm sorry, we don't all choose Jesus as the main thrust and focus. My old denomination in Canada worshiped the law and prophecy far more than Jesus.

Choosing Jesus is choosing life.

The bread of life – John 6:35, 48

The living bread – John 6:51

Whoever eats my flesh and drinks my blood has eternal life – John 6:53

I am the resurrection and the life – John 11:25

I am the way the truth and the life – John 14:6

The Messiah – John 4:26

The light – John 9:5

The Gate – John 10:7

The son of God – John 10:36

The Lord – John 13:13

The Vine – John15:1

The Alpha and the Omega – Rev. 1:8, 17

It is by focusing on Jesus and making him the very center of our lives that we will find life, and escape the thinking of the tree of the knowledge of good and evil. When you choose life, you are choosing a whole new way to think – one not taught at seminary. When you choose life, you are choosing the deepest form of repentance.

An old definition of repentance is, "turn and go the other way." Turning and going the other way is a by-product of repentance, not repentance itself. We need a new way of thinking. We need a renewing of the mind.

Remember the motor boat story from chapter 12 defining repentance? If you have a motor boat with an auto-pilot set to south, you can grab the steering wheel and turn the direction around to north. As long as you exert effort (self-will) and determination you can keep the boat going north. At some point you are going to get tired or bored or fed-up exerting effort to force the boat to go north. At some point you let go of the steering wheel and instantly the auto-pilot turns the boat south. The "mind" of the boat had remained the same even when a will was exerted to force a different direction. What is needed is to reprogram the auto-pilot (renew the mind) and then it becomes ten times easier to travel in the correct direction. Repentance is a change of mind – and the change of direction is a fruit or by-product of that change (renewing).

Here is where an accurate understanding of the new covenant is so important. The new heart and the renewed mind are *the work of God*, not the fruit of our silly religious behavior modification programs. Remember Jeremiah 31? God makes it clear in the new covenant He would be doing these wonderful works of putting a new mind and heart in us, and writing His laws on our new heart. This is the work of His spirit, which is the reason why we must learn to rest in His spirit (Matt. 11:28-31) and simply focus on life, not endless debates about right and wrong, good and evil.

When we choose the Tree of Life (and don't assume you already have) we are choosing a whole new way *to think, relate and minister*. We are choosing a deep form of repentance that opens a new door to life than may be beyond what our hurting, burned-out, cynical, angry heart and mind can presently understand. Repent of being an expert in right and wrong, and chose life my friend.

NOTES:

NOTES:

NOTES:

Chapter 18

The Tree of Life and Healing

In burnout one of the frequent questions asked is, "Will I ever heal? Will I ever recover and have interest and zeal again?"

The answer is yes, it is possible, but, some do not and keep spiraling downward into a black abyss. By staying in the bitterness and sour spirit of the tree of the knowledge of good and evil, death keeps flowing through our spirit. You can mechanically get down on your knees and pray for those who are your enemies, but if you are praying this way from the tree of the knowledge of good and evil, it will still leave you unhealed and frustrated.

Let me illustrate an idea with a mountaineering story. When you are climbing in most mountain ranges in the world, you can sit down and rest when you are tired. As you take a breather, drink some water and scarf down a power bar, your body is recovering. The blood is removing the lactic acid from your leg muscles, and your heart and lungs are adapting to the altitude. Recovery is occurring; it is just a matter of time.

However, when you climb in the Himalayas, the tallest mountains on earth, you pass through a boundary at 24,000 feet. Once you are past this point you have entered the death zone. Above 24,000 feet the body does not recover. Even when you stop to rest, and have a drink, your body is slowly dying. It still feels good to sit down and chew on a snack, but your body is still slowly dying. Even if you never jumped up and started plodding higher up the mountain, your body would slow down and deteriorate to the point of death. Life in the *death zone*, no matter how picturesque the clouds below you are, no matter how good the camaraderie with team mates, no matter how good the rest feels or snack tastes, no matter how beautiful the scenery – staying in the *death zone* leads to death!

Sounds a lot like the tree of the knowledge of good and evil doesn't it? No matter how good the good may seem in the tree of the knowledge of good and evil, it leads to death. No matter how much you read the Bible, if you are reading it from the tree of the knowledge of good and evil perspective, seeking to be an expert in right and wrong, you will still die. No matter how many extra hours a day you pray, if you pray out of the tree of the knowledge of good and evil perspective, you will still die. The Pharisee who fasted twice a week and thanked God he was not like other men is a classic example of the tree of the knowledge of good and evil thinking and praying. So what does this mean regarding healing?

"*Then the angel showed me the river of water of life, as clear as crystal, flowing from the throne of God and the Lamb down the middle of the great street of the city. On each side of the river stood a tree of life, bearing twelve crops of fruit, yielding its fruit for every month. And the leaves of the tree are for the healing of the nations.*" Revelation 22:1-2 NIV.

It may seem like an oversimplification, but living in the tree of death leads to death, living in the tree of life leads to life. If you truly want to heal, and feel good about life, God, family and church again, you need to live in Life. You need to eat the right fruit. Sure, you can go to a $200 an hour therapist until you run out of money, and it may feel very good. Someone is listening to you and not judging you. It feels good to unload and talk freely. But if you still hang out in the tree of the knowledge of good and evil, can a $200 therapist completely heal you? *Can you live in the death zone and be healed?*

Plunge into the tree of life, and if you need to, find a therapist who also lives in the tree of life, and you will be well on your way! What you will learn, the new way you will think, the new approach toward your enemies, the way you will relate to others and God, the whole new life-giving attitude you will have will lead to life and heal you to bear much good fruit along the way! Tthe rest of this book is designed to help you better understand what tree of life living is all about. Much of it has to do with the life flow of blood covenant love.

Remember how David approached Mephibosheth, his enemy? David spoke life to Mephibosheth. David breathed blood covenant love into Mephibosheth. A new heart and mind started to develop in Mephibosheth. He started to take on the very spirit of his covenant representative, Jonathan. That is healing.

Merely resting physically for a few weeks and then jumping back into the same grind and performing ministry the way you always have is not an answer. That's why at our retreat ranch for burned out leaders and church members we teach the principles in this book so that the recovering individual can return to service, but from the tree of life. Living in the tree of life is an ongoing process of healing from the taint of the world.

Get out of the death zone! Humble yourself down to a lower elevation where the air is thicker, and fill your heart and lungs with Life!

NOTES:

NOTES:

NOTES:

Chapter 19

Abigail's Strategy

"Now think it over and see what you can do, because disaster is hanging over our master and his whole household. He is such a wicked man that no one can talk to him." (I Sam. 25:17 NIV)

We often receive calls and e-mails from the wives of pastors or leaders who are feeling the pain and pressure of their mate's burn-out. They are doing all they can think of to preserve what peace is left and keep things in their lives from falling completely apart. They are well aware that something is wrong and are desperately searching for a cure. As wise women of faith they search the scriptures, pray, surf the internet looking for ministries that can put a name to what they are experiencing. They are caught in the vortex of their husband's torture as he searches his soul for his own answers. It is lonely for both of them.

Abigail must have been a lonely wife as she watched her husband spiral downward in his self-satisfaction, taking those around him for granted. The scripture says that he was a very wealthy man, but cruel and mean in his dealings. He held a banquet and presided over it as if he were a king. At the banquet he was in high spirits and drunk. These are a few of his personality characteristics. He took care of himself and did not repay good from others with good. His pride and vanity are called foolish. He was considered a fool, which is his name, Nabal.

As the Proverbs speak to us, there are people who won't listen to reason or wisdom. They are fools. It is very difficult to live with a foolish person. "*Whoever corrects a mocker invites insult; whoever rebukes a wicked man incurs abuse. Do not rebuke a mocker or he will hate you; rebuke a wise man and he will love you*" (Proverbs 9:7-8. NIV)

The whole account is quite a story. David and his men were outcasts living in the desert and hill country of Israel. They helped their fellow Israelites against marauders, Philistines, Amalekites, and other enemies while at the same time they were trying to stay one step ahead of King Saul who sought to kill David. These men protected rich Nabal's shepherds and flocks while they were in his part of the country. They never took meat for themselves nor did any harm to the servants of Nabal. They were like a wall of protection to that rich man.

When Nabal went out to the countryside to watch the shearing of his three thousand sheep, David heard about it and sent ten men to convey messages of blessing –"*Long life to you! Good health to you and your household! And good health to all that is yours!*" They spoke of the protection they had been affording the shepherds and flocks and then asked for whatever food he (Nabal) could find for them. Their hearts were right and they came to do good to this man.

Nabal answered their request with insults against David. He acted as if he had never heard of this great warrior of Israel whom Samuel had anointed to be the next king and who had killed Goliath and many other Philistine enemies.

David was not impressed. In fact, he commanded his men to put on their swords! And four hundred men armed themselves to follow David to this slaughter. Justice must be done! But is that God's plan or David's?

One very smart servant ran to tell Nabal's wife about the insulting manner in which David's men had been treated and how they had really been a big help to all of them. The servant knew that she was a wise woman for he said, *"Now think it over and see what you can do, because disaster is hanging over our master and his whole household. He is such a wicked man that no one can talk to him.*" What would you have done if some servant was saying that about your husband?

"*Abigail lost no time.*" This woman did not go into a panic, did not start crying about the disaster that was eminent, and did not run to hide. She took stock of what was on hand – two hundred loaves of bread, two skins of wine, five dressed sheep, a bushel of roasted grain, cakes of raisins and cakes of figs. (She didn't forget dessert!) They quickly loaded the food on donkeys and she told the servants to go on ahead, she would follow. But she did not tell her husband, Nabal. Of course, he would not have allowed her to go and feed David and his men when he had spoken such evil against them.

Abigail was looking to the higher good. We are all familiar with the precept that a woman should be in submission to her husband. Pleasing her husband was a good thing but when disaster was looming she used her own wisdom to forestall it. The whole farm operation was at stake, the lives of all the servants, her own life and of course, her husband's life were in danger.

Abigail decided to go straight to the person who had been insulted and see if she could apologize. There was a chance that David would not accept her apology and she would be killed by the sword herself. But she felt that perhaps he was not as hard-hearted as her own husband. Perhaps he would listen if she humbled herself and appealed to his desire to please God.

The Proverbs were written many years after this event but perhaps Solomon was looking at some of the historical events of David's life when he penned Proverbs 6:2-5, "*if you have been trapped by what you said, ensnared by the words of your mouth, then do this, my son, to free yourself, since you have fallen into your neighbor's hands: Go and humble yourself; press your plea with your neighbor! Allow no sleep to your eyes, no slumber to your eyelids. Free yourself like a gazelle from the hand of the hunter, like a bird from the snare of the fowler.*" (NIV)

Abigail's strategy was to send the gift ahead of her, to set the stage, to humble herself, realizing that David was the leader of a sizeable army, a powerful man, anointed to be king, and to appeal to his conscience and commitment to God. She chose to appeal to the life of God in David and fight the spirit of death which seemed imminent. This was truly a visible life and death choice.

She hit the nail on the head. David received the food for his men, his anger subsided and he praised God that she had prevented him from avenging himself. Disaster was averted... this time.

Many women have a sixth sense that trouble is in the wind. God seems to have blessed the weaker sex with the ability to read people especially those who have influence over family members. When women feel the family members are endangered they go into high gear to protect them. Ladies who would never raise their voices under normal circumstances can shout down a football team if they feel a child is threatened. When crisis rears its head wise women go into action to preserve lives and keep the family together. Abigail acted out of hope and faith that there was a way out, an answer to the inevitable. God was with her and she succeeded in turning David's heart away from justly punishing her husband. Abigail, by humbling herself, spoke life into David's heart that changed history. She was doing it to preserve her husband and household but it worked to preserve David and the whole nation. Perhaps David would have been punished by God for taking justice into his own hands, as he was later on in his reign as king.

It was far better for God to be the one to mete out punishment than to have a mere man do so. David himself voiced that when God offered him a choice of punishments for numbering the people of Israel. (I Chronicles 21) He said, "*I am in deep distress. Let me fall into the hands of the LORD, for his mercy is very great; but do not let me fall into the hands of men.*" The ensuing plague of the Lord took the lives of seventy thousand men of Israel then the Lord said, "*Enough*!" Wow! That was a horrible punishment on the whole nation! It would seem that David expected a worse punishment if it were by the hands of men.

Nabal did not get out of the situation unscathed even though his dear wife had interceded to save his skin. Abigail came home with the servants and empty donkeys to find her husband holding a feast in the house, in high spirits and very drunk. He was oblivious to the horrors that he had just been spared. Poor man! Abigail chose to go to her room and say nothing until morning. I'm sure she was mulling over what to say, and how to say it. This man was known for his violent temper and irrational behavior. At least everyone in the household knew his true nature. Now, what could she do to prevent him from turning on her when he knew the truth?

Perhaps Abigail knew Nabal's weak point. No doubt he was suffering from a hangover the next morning after being "very drunk" the night before. She got up at daybreak and told him "all these things". She told him about the army of men who were on their way to their house yesterday and how she and the servants had greeted them with food to prevent them descending on the property with swords unsheathed ready to slaughter everyone. She told of how David had graciously received the food and told his men to call off the battle. She told of how God had turned David's heart away from revenge on Nabal.

This report must have devastated the pride of Nabal. He was so shocked at the news that his "heart failed him and he became as stone". Yes, pride comes before a fall. Nabal may have slightly recovered, we don't know. For ten days Abigail must have suffered with the anger and spite of her husband. The account says that ten days later, the Lord struck Nabal and he died. So, Abigail didn't have to take all the blame for her husband's death. The Lord brought upon him the punishment deserved for his long history of mistreating other people and indulging himself.

There is a time for a woman, a wife, to reach out for help for the sake of her family. When disaster looms is not the time to be proud and silent. It is the time to cry out to God and to those who can help in the time of need. Even if she is alone in seeking counsel, she should. She can ask for prayer, counsel on what she can do, and for support. In the church we always assume that the family is a good one until it falls apart. But, we are all in the battle against Satan and the world every day. We all battle human nature. Humans fail, daily. Marriages fail, daily, in the church. Leaders fall and need to be lifted up. "No man is an island. No man stands alone," says the old folk song. Yet, it seems to be such a shame in the church to cry out for help. We need to make it less shameful and more productive to state the facts of our weakness in the church with impunity. We need to bear one another's burdens instead of making them a reason to destroy one another.

The end result of Abigail's strategy was that by wisdom her household had been spared and she came to the attention of the next king of Israel. David praised God that he had not been the one who punished Nabal and that God had upheld David's cause after all by punishing David's enemies. David saw Abigail as a good ally to have on his side and a wise partner for his life's work. He asked her to marry him.

To the servants who came conveying the message to Abigail

she bowed down with her face to the ground. (She seemed to esteem others as better than herself.) Her words were, "*Here is your maidservant, ready to serve you and wash the feet of my master's servants.*" She quickly got on her donkey and commanded her five maidservants to come along. What did she really know about this man David except that he listened to reason and to God and that he had command over quite an army of renegades? Yet, she seemed ready to trust God and set off on another adventure.

This lady, Abigail, made quick decisions at all the crucial points of her story. She used her resources where they would serve the most people. She did not cower in fear of her ruthless husband. She knew how to humble herself. She knew how to ask for help. She was easy for her servants to approach. She was a woman of action, not just thought. These were all part of her strategy to solve family and community problems. She would be a great church leader today. To have more Abigails in all congregations would change the face of the church. God bless all of you Abigails out there. We need you to speak life and covenant love into the spirits of all believers. We need you to preserve all that is good and beautiful in the Bride of Christ and not allow foolishness to have sway over the Church.

NOTES:

NOTES:

NOTES:

Chapter 20

Tree of Life – Practical Application

Since living in the tree of the knowledge of good and evil is so natural to human nature, and is so prevalent in our society, what does tree of life living look like in everyday application?

When you live in the tree of life you walk in a simple, childlike innocence. You are not an expert in right and wrong, good and evil. You have a childlike approach to life and relationships. The characteristics that come with the tree of the knowledge of good and evil, which are – see, know, judge and blame – are not a part of your personality or life style.

When you meet people, you have a beaming smile on your face, not a frown of evaluation and caution. But it's not a painted on Christian smile, but, rather, the result of the flow of blood covenant love in your spirit. When you open your mouth and speak, words of life come out, even when speaking with someone who greatly dislikes you. You speak words of life because it leads to life; life in your enemy, and life in your own spirit. You avoid gossip because it leads to death. You speak the truth because it leads to life, and lying leads to death.

Everything you do leads to life in you and in others. You avoid those things that are very common but lead you or others toward death. When you are accused by others, you speak blessings into their lives. When a staff member does something wrong you work with them in love and bless them and love them into better service. You don't get into mini sermons on right and wrong and moralizing until the staff member decides working in another church would be fun.

When the worship leader forgets his guitar, you don't get angry or frustrated. You speak life into him and into the congregation, and then get on with worshiping God which leads to life. How church service "looks" that morning is not important, and certainly doesn't affect your image.

The main issue here is life. Making life choices in thousands of decisions everyday, is tree of life living. It may seem natural to accuse your teen of laziness when you find the sink still full of dishes, but does accusing lead to life when we may not know the whole story? And, even if you guess correctly, a brow beating of your teen may not lead to better dishwasher. Even in correction we should try and find a way of speaking life into a person. God created all people with this desperate need for real life, worth, purpose. The truly powerful leader is one who knows how to speak life into the very spirit of the person they are trying to motivate. The weak leader resorts to attack, belittling and hurting to coerce the person into action. Most definitely, that is the tree of the knowledge of good and evil.

Maybe you're a youth pastor, and you are upset at a young man in your group who shows up for services with more body piercing than a Spanish bull near the end of a bullfight! So are you going to speak life into him? Or allow your worries about how it makes your youth group look cause you to try and control and brow beat him? Life or death; that's what it is about. If you go off running around worrying about right and wrong, good and evil, you will wear out and burnout in due time.

Life and death. Life does not come from expertise in good and evil, but, it does come from the revelation of life and death. Life flow comes from Life himself, Jesus. His blood covenant love flows to us – if we will let it – and impacts our spirits such that we take on his attitudes and love for others. We become conduits for the flow of life to others. Unless you and I can understand this, we should not re-enter ministry. Unless we can understand this we will never be life-giving ministry leaders.

Everything we do and say should be because those actions or statements lead to life. We should not do and say things because we are angry, insulted, embarrassed, fearful, intimidated or wounded.

Everything should lead to life. Even tithing. Why do you tithe? Because God commands it? Because your denomination teaches so? Because it sets the right example? Because if you don't God will fry you in hell? Because there is a big fat promise in Malachi of blessings and you want to cash in? Or, do you tithe because it leads to life in you and others? Do you tithe because being a cheerful giver leads to life?

One reason tithing and giving of offerings can be such a sensitive issue in some groups is because the idea of it being life giving to others and themselves is not understood. For many, giving up "their" hard earned money is an obligation and must be done or else – God or church will be angry with them. They have a slave mentality toward a life-giving practice.

It's true, being a cheerful giver in any area of life leads to life. Writing a nice big fat tithe check on Sunday morning with deep regret in your heart only leads to death in your spirit.

The innocence in the tree of life comes from knowing Jesus personally. The purely intellectual believer who knows much about Jesus, but doesn't know Jesus from the heart will find it impossible to walk in this type of innocence. When you have this innocence, the anointing can flow freely. Without this innocence, well, knowledge is all you have.

Since it is all about life and death, how can we tell if we are living in the tree of life? With time, and understanding that it is a heart issue, you will know easily. Here is one interesting test. How do you react to other people's sin? Do you respond with life? If you do, you will experience something Jesus died to give us – freedom! If you respond with a sour spirit to their sin or your own sin, then you have eaten of the wrong tree. If your response is free from victimization, you are well on the road to the tree of life.

NOTES:

NOTES:

NOTES:

Chapter 21

Tree of Life – Matter of Heart

In the table below we attempt to give you an idea of the differences between the two trees. Really what we are talking about *is a matter of heart; a direction of spirit.* Two believers can look exactly the same, carrying out the same activity, but one may live in the tree of the knowledge of good and evil and the other in the tree of life. One's efforts will be a blessing of life to those around them, the other will radiate death to those around them. Use this simple table to help you get the gist of the differences. The table in no way represents actions cast in stone. ***To think of certain actions as defining the two trees is a big mistake.*** These are simple examples to help you get the feel of the tree of life; an aid to catch the direction of the spirit of each tree. Please let me repeat myself. **The difference between the two trees is a way of thinking, a direction of spirit.** The difference is a way of seeing, a world view, and an overall approach to live through that view. The tree of life is a worldview or life-view where we practically believe light will overcome darkness, good will overcome evil, love will overcome hate, peace will overcome war, forgiveness will overcome bitterness.

Tree of Life – Leads to Life

Tree of the Knowledge of Good and Evil – Leads to Death

The reason the Tree of life promotes life is because it points to life Himself. When we speak life, act life, serve life to others, we are touching their very spirit, as well as their heart. The very life flow of God is touching them. The flow of blood covenant love is entering their being, and impacting their heart and spirit. That promotes life in us also because life has flowed through us to others.

Death is another story. When we move in the tree of the knowledge of good and evil we are heading for death even when it seems so logical that we are doing what is good. Remember, in the tree of the knowledge of good and evil, even good leads to death. Amazing! Shocking! Evil also leads to death! So, put it together: Good leads to death, being preoccupied with right and wrong leads to death, evil leads to death. But, life leads to real life in others and ourselves.

Tree of Life Values – Flow of Life Changes People from the Inside Out.

Tree of the Knowledge of Good and Evil Values – See, Know, Judge, Blame toward self and others.

The flesh finds judging and blaming others a natural automatic activity. Speaking death to others becomes an unrecognized natural way of speaking in both business and family. Humor on TV and in movies becomes based on this way of thinking. It is a natural part of the lost person's world view.

The tree of life individual believes that in the end, truth triumphs over falsehood, right triumphs over wrong, good triumphs over evil, love triumphs over hate. The values of the tree of life individual allow him to relax and trust God because of these triumphs. This person knows the flow of blood covenant love can change hearts and spirits.

Tree of Life – Bless and Forgive

Tree of the Knowledge of Good and Evil – Hold a Grudge and Justify

In the tree of life we are not interested in "who's done wrong" but rather, how can we bless and speak life into a person or a situation. We want to promote life, and the flow of God's life to others. We will forgive and move on. We will bless those who curse us. We will bless those who spitefully use us.

In the tree of the knowledge of good and evil, we tend to get very angry at those who hurt us. We blame them. We hold them responsible for our unhappiness. Even if we made a mistake, it is their fault we are in pain right now. They are to blame!

Tree of Life – Accept Responsibility

Tree of the Knowledge of Good and Evil – Displace Responsibility

The first two humans who ate from the tree of the knowledge of good and evil pointed their fingers at someone else for their misfortune. Humans had never done that before. Lucifer had. Suddenly instead of supporting and helping one another as they had in their short past, they now were placing responsibility on another and claiming innocence for themselves. What a sad scenario.

When you live in the tree of life you accept responsibility regardless of the circumstances. You are now a new creation in Christ, and the fact your mother or father mistreated you when you were a child is a sad fact, but it is no longer an excuse for you. You are new in Jesus and must go forward and do the life-giving thing, and move on. Finger pointing and blaming others is counter productive.

Tree of Life – Live in Freedom

Tree of the Knowledge of Good and Evil – Live in Victimization

When you *do not* point the finger of blame at another, when you *do not* displace responsibility, but rather, take responsibility for yourself completely, you experience a freedom that you can only enjoy when you are in a close walk with the Lord Jesus. You look to Him with optimism, not your enemies with blame. The spirit dimension is the limit, not the earthly lows of blaming and condemning others for your problems.

Victimization is the deepest prison anyone in the tree of the knowledge of good and evil can ever live in. It is a state of hopelessness.

Tree of Life – Flow in Unconditional Love

Tree of the Knowledge of Good and Evil – Struggle in Fear

Tree of Lifers come to know and understand Father's unconditional love and they rejoice. They walk in love and the freedom Jesus won them, and the wrong kind of fear is not in the equation.

Tree of the knowledge of good and evil people are very concerned about right and wrong and pleasing God, and have a fear that they are not measuring up. If they are not blessed it simply must mean they are failing in some area. Life becomes a guessing game on how to please God and avoid the fear of failure.

Tree of Life – Accepting, Believing the Best

Tree of the Knowledge of Good and Evil – Evaluating, Suspicious

Is the glass half full or half empty? When one of your major purposes in life is to speak and convey life to everyone around you, you tend to see the bright side of all circumstances. You know even if things are looking grim, by speaking the flow of God's life into a situation, it can only get better. You realize the most powerful force there is, is God's love and all it can accomplish against human odds. When you live in the tree of life you are not naive, thinking everybody honest and fair. You know they are human, and human nature can be horrid. But, with the wisdom of a serpent, and the kindness and gentleness of a dove, you move through life carefully, but positively, because you know God is sovereign and His plan is going to succeed even if the glass is half empty!

In the tree of the knowledge of good and evil you are the expert in right and wrong, and you can see wrong far too clearly in everyone else. You become suspicious. You see others as sinners and failures rather than future children of God who are a work in progress. You're the guy or gal who says, "Watch out for Christians, they will rip you off as fast as anyone!"

Tree of Life – Positive and Encouraging

Tree of the Knowledge of Good and Evil – Critical and Cynical

With the very life flow of God inside them, tree of lifers naturally speak the words that make for life in another's spirit. They are acutely aware of the proverbs that speak about words containing life or death.

Again, it sounds repetitive, but in the tree of the knowledge of good and evil where your focus is often right and wrong, what can I do and what can't I do, you become critical of others who do the things you can't, and in time this gives way to cynicism. Elijah stomping around in the desert saying to himself repeatedly that he was the only faithful one left and everyone else in Israel was a loser is a classic example. God had to remind him there were at least seven thousand others who had never bent the knee to Baal.

Tree of Life – Concerned about Life and Death Issues

Tree of the Knowledge Good and Evil – Concerned about Right and Wrong

Jesus was so concerned that the lost should hear the message of life, he hung out with the biggest sinners in town. He was frequently invited over to their homes for meals and fellowship. He was not overly concerned with their outward appearance and immediate short comings. He knew all things would be taken care of in due time. What mattered was speaking life and love into their being, so that their focus was redirected, and their understanding corrected. Jesus accepted them where the lost presently were, and loved them in a direction toward the Kingdom.

The tree of the knowledge of good and evil fellow is very concerned with how circumstances look right now, and he is often self-absorbed wondering how he and others are measuring up in God's eyes.

Tree of Life – Walk in Innocence/Anointing Flows

Tree of the Knowledge of Good and Evil – Walk in a Competitive Spirit

The tree of life pastor doesn't try to make things happen. He leaves that to God. He, his mate and the other leaders in the congregation simply walk with the faithful innocence Adam and Eve had in the garden. God is in charge, and let's get out of the way and let the Holy Spirit do the driving. These men and women are not concerned with how others view them. They stand up and preach life-giving sermons week after week in a childlike innocence, and if someone's church is growing at a faster pace than theirs, well, so be it, praise God.

Leaders in the tree of the knowledge of good and evil can be very competitive. So competitive it often leads to congregational or denominational politics that are so ugly I don't want to talk about it! Church splits and gossip and destruction of the body of Christ are often the products.

Tree of Life – Give People their Freedom

Tree of the Knowledge of Good and Evil – Controlling, Manipulating, Micro-managing

No one really tries to escape America. Some threaten to move away before each Presidential election if their candidate doesn't get elected! But one problem America does have, is illegal immigrants sneaking *into* America. They want in because there is freedom here in America. Your creativity and innovation has no limits in America. You can come from a poor country, and become anything you dream of in America! So it is in a church living in the tree of life. People are not micro-managed, but rather, have freedom to develop, be creative, and jump into innovative ministries that help the community.

When a church is micro-managed by a control freak pastor, he will need to build a Berlin wall around the church to keep the people in! Often the tree of the knowledge of good and evil leader doesn't think of the people as a work in progress. Rather, he often is trying to make them over into his own image. He usually doesn't realize this fact.

Tree of Life – Let others have Responsibility for Themselves

Tree of the Knowledge of Good and Evil – Feel Responsible for Others – Interfere.

We love and want to help the children of God, but, we can't live their lives for them. The tree of the knowledge of good and evil leader doesn't know that. He's the interfering fixer of everyone's problem and concern. It is all part of his concern about how the church "looks."

The tree of life leader lovingly preaches and teaches the word of God, but he also leaves a lot for Jesus to do for each person. After all, it is Jesus' church!

Tree of Life – Give People the Freedom to Develop God's Gifts in their Lives and Ministry.

Tree of the Knowledge of Good and Evil – Others must do it Your Way – the Only Way.

The tree of life pastor becomes a coach to help every member develop their gifts and ministries. He or she is an encourager, a trouble shooter in fine tuning members' ministries. But he is not a dictator.

For the tree of the knowledge of good and evil leader, there is only one way to do something. His way. After all he is the ordained leader. If you don't do it his way you are in rebellion against God's authority! His leadership crushes creativity and innovation. People with new ideas become discouraged and head for the back door. If the tree of the knowledge of good and evil leader does agree to do something like a small group ministry, he will write a two inch thick manual for all small group leaders to follow to the letter, that way he is still in control even if he can't be present to micro-manage!

Tree of Life – An easy loving Sweet Spirit

Tree of the Knowledge of Good and Evil – A Sour Spirit, Controlling, Selfish, Suspicious.

When right and wrong and impressing God *are not the main focus* of your life, you can relax and be kind and gentle to all people. You're not hung up on "getting it right' or making others get it right. You love people, teach them the truth, and leave the rest to Jesus. Everyone is a work in progress, and that progress is according to Father's time table, not yours!

The tree of the knowledge of good and evil leader may appear very kind and loving on the outside, but inside he or she wants the development and progress of others according to their own timetable. They often become frustrated when people don't respond to their personal wishes. They become depressed when the attendance at mid-week Bible study isn't what the leader thinks it should be!

Tree of Life – A Helpful Attitude

Tree of the Knowledge of Good and Evil – A Finger-pointing Spirit

A church member presents a personal problem. The tree of life leader is helpful and patient. The member's problem or failure is not a reflection on his pastoring abilities. He cares and does what he can to promote life and direction in the member's life.

The tree of the knowledge of good and evil leader points out why the member is having problems with their teens. He has the answers, and he isn't afraid to point the finger of blame on the dad, and tell him he's blown his child rearing. The leader justifies treating the member this way by saying he will not compromise with the truth! "I will teach what is true even if it hurts. I will not be a wishy-washy pastor!" Then the tree of the knowledge of good and evil leader wonders why the member will never come to him again for advice!

Tree of Life – Speaking Words of Life

Tree of the Knowledge of Good and Evil – Speaking Sarcasm, Suspicion, Defeat.

People love talking to someone who lives in the tree of life. Somehow it is so encouraging, yet realistic at the same time. Their words are not exaggerating, but they are filled with hope and inspiration. They remind us of God's purpose and all that Jesus did for us, and we walk away knowing Jesus will finish what he started in us. Their speech is not filled with why America is going down the tubes, and how everyone at work is a liar and a thief. Nor is their speech filled with who did what wrong at church last week, or how the church would grow faster if we had a decent pastor! That's talk for the other tree!

Tree of Life – Allowing Differences of Opinion, even Different Interpretations of Scripture in non-Salvation Issues

Tree of the Knowledge of God and Evil – Believing or Teaching Your Interpretation as an Absolute

The tree of lifer can sit down in a donut shop with another believer from another church and have a grand conversation and wonderful fellowship, because they focus on the absolutes of scripture; the salvation issues. They don't get hung up on different church cultures and interpretations. If they pray in tongues and the other person doesn't, it's no big deal. Speaking life into the other is more important.

The tree of the knowledge of good and evil fellow may not even show up at the donut shop depending on what his church teaches about the sin of eating donuts!

Tree of Life – Focus on the Absolutes of Scripture (heaven and hell issues)

Tree of the Knowledge of Good and Evil – Make Life and Death issues out of Everything You Believe

The tree of the knowledge of good and evil fellow places everything he believes inside the circle he might call true Christianity. If you don't fit inside that circle, you may not be in the Kingdom of God. But what if you have a different interpretation on a non-salvation issue? To the tree of the knowledge of good and evil fellow there may not be such a thing as a non-salvation issue! Everything, including which translation of the Bible you read may have to do with salvation!

Tree of Life – Focus Teaching on Life and Jesus Himself

Tree of the Knowledge of Good and Evil – Focus Teaching on Right and Wrong

When you are hung up on pleasing and impressing God, you end up focused on fence laws. You don't ask, "How can I keep the law?" Rather you think in terms of, "What can I do and what can't I do?"

The tree of lifer lives in the reality of two things. Love God and love your fellow man. Living in the tree of life accomplishes both. Decisions are made based on ways and means of loving people toward the Kingdom. Decisions are made by asking if this or that leads to life. Right and wrong, good and evil still exist to the tree of life fellow, but that is not their focus. Promoting life is the focus.

Tree of Life – Believers fall in love with Jesus – Read their Bibles and Pray with great Joy

Tree of Knowledge of Good and Evil – Religious approach to Prayer and Study

In the tree of life the believer falls head over heels in love with Jesus, and the resulting by-product is a great enthusiasm for knowing Jesus better. They love their Bibles and love reading and praying because it draws them closer to their King.

People in the tree of the knowledge of good and evil read and study because it is a good Christian discipline. The pastor said good Christians read their Bibles so you read your Bible, but it can become a chore instead of a joy.

Tree of Life – Use Bible to bring Joy and Hope to Others

Tree of the Knowledge of Good and Evil – Use Bible as a Weapon of Tyranny to show failure in People's Lives

The Bible can be a wonderful book of life to the lost, or it can be a weapon of tyranny in the hands of someone whose focus is right and wrong. In the hands of this type of person, the Bible becomes the source of knowledge upon which the seeing- knowing- judging-blaming value system is based. The tree of the knowledge of good and evil person uses their Bible to turn people away with their judging, self-righteous approach. We can use the Bible to turn people on to God, or turn them off Christianity forever!

Tree of Life – Church Board – Proactive Support of Pastor

Tree of the Knowledge of Good and Evil – Board becomes Self-Serving god

Probably any form of church government will work, ***if,*** everybody in authority lives in the tree of life. A board operating in the tree of life has deep respect and Godly fear of the office God created called, "Pastor." They work with the pastor, not against him, and they do so in a manner that promotes life. Even when there is disagreement over a plan or an approach, the meetings are handled in a life-giving manner.

There is no talk behind the pastor's back. There are no huddles in the dark parking lot after the board has left the church and the pastor is not present. God help any pastor who has tree of the knowledge of good and evil people on his board. Let the power struggles begin!

Tree of Life – Parents who Communicate Love and Acceptance to Children

Tree of the Knowledge of Good and Evil – Parents making Right and Wrong more Important than Relationship

When your parents had to correct you as a child, were you left with the assurance they loved you and you would always be their child? I hope so. Or, after the tongue lashing, were you left thinking your parents cared more about other peoples' opinions and feelings than your own? Did you feel they might disown you someday?

Tree of Life – A Genuine Unconditional Love for People

Tree of the Knowledge of Good and Evil – An Inner Contempt for People

Some people in leadership don't really love people. They have a problem with people never measuring up to expectations. Deep inside they come to resent people.

The tree of life individual comes to love people in a simple manner. The flow of God's love into them causes a real love for others, despite the fact people do disappoint them. The flow of life and blood covenant love does make all the difference.

Tree of Life – Lifestyle of Giving

Tree of the Knowledge of Good and Evil – Lifestyle of Getting that is Disguised as Giving

When life and blood covenant love is pouring into you, the most natural response becomes giving away. You live by the philosophy "what's mine is yours." In the story of the Lost Son in Luke chapter 15, the Father lives by this philosophy.

The younger son lives by the idea, "what's yours is mine." His older brother who gets so upset with the younger returning to the farm lives by the philosophy, "what's mine is mine." Only the Father in the story lives in the tree of life.

In the tree of life we come to understand we can not out-give our Father. There is no need to hoard. The more we give away, the more the Father fills us with His love and life.

Tree of Life – Live in the New Way of the Spirit

Tree of the Knowledge of Good and Evil – Live in the Old Way of the Written Code

Even for the modern legalist who claims to be living in the New Covenant, you will find a whole list of do's and don'ts because of the focus on right and wrong, good and evil. It is important to impress God so the blessings will flow.

In the tree of life the individual understands there is a new approach, a new way to relate to God. It is no longer performance based religion. It is now love and relationship. God blesses us because he loves us. We now learn to rest in His very Spirit (Matt 11:28) and allow the Holy Spirit to lead us. We are now life and love oriented, not performance based. We walk in the spirit, not in a behavior modification program of do's and don'ts.

Tree of Life – Giving Congregation Freedom – Respecting their Adult Decisions

Tree of the Knowledge of Good and Evil – Keeping an Attendance Sheet at church and calling everyone on Monday to see why they were not in church Sunday

The control freak leader is the one most likely to burnout, and drives everyone away from himself. In the tree of life we respect people's decisions, even if we disagree with their opinions. We simply can't live other people's lives for them. Remember, God does not force us to do anything. He gives us lots of space, and he allows us to reap what we sow. We must do the same. Our job as believers is to love people into the direction of life.

Tree of Life – Jesus' words and actions working with the Woman caught in Adultery

Tree of the Knowledge of Good and Evil – Pharisees words and motives regarding Woman caught in Adultery

The Pharisees were technically correct. The law was clear regarding adultery. The penalty was death by stoning. Jesus worked within the framework of the law and gave the Pharisees the right to stone her. He simply asked that it be done in a certain order, starting with the Pharisee who had never sinned.

What is truly exciting to notice is how Jesus worked with this lady caught in great sin. First he writes or draws on the ground, pulling the leering eyes of the men off the woman, who was probably just wrapped in a blanket. Then, at the end he turned to her and made two life-giving statements. "Neither do I accuse you." "Go and sin no more." His actions and his words spoke life into this woman. There was no brow beating. No lecture on how she was ruining her life, her marriage and disgracing her children. Those would be natural consequences of her actions. Jesus spoke life to this woman to give her hope for the future.

I think you get the gist of it. Remember, we are not really talking about a set of behaviors. We are talking about two ways of thinking. Two attitudes toward life; two philosophical views toward the same events in life: one way of thinking inspired by love and the Holy Spirit, the other way of thinking driven by the darkness of human nature disguised by noble ideals.

The best way to move into the Tree of Life is to learn to "rest" in the very spirit of Jesus. Fully stepping into the New Covenant means entering into a rest in Jesus' spirit, and moving away from living half in the old way of the written code and half in the new way of the spirit. In the next chapter we will explore this idea.

NOTES:

NOTES:

NOTES:

Chapter 22

Rest in the Spirit

Without a doubt, part of the key to learning to live in the tree of life is to learn to **"rest"** in the very spirit of Jesus Christ. When we are weary, heavily burdened by religion, Jesus calls us to himself and promises us *rest.* Why, why, why is rest an action verb for so many leaders and believers? Where did we get the idea we had to save the church and the world? Yes, we are the body of Christ. We are His ambassadors. But unless we do this work in His power, it will not succeed. Here's a statement to chew on. *Unless we stop working so hard and learn how to rest, nothing will get done!*

Jesus was serious. As long as we, with our wonderful driven personalities, keep striving and trying to do it all by our own strength, we can never rest in His spirit. We will run by our own resources until we come to an end of ourselves, and burn out. At Smoldering Wick Ministries we view burnout as a blessing, for this very reason. It forces us to rest and allows the power of God to flow.

I grew up in the Canadian Rockies, and our family also lived in Colorado for three years. I have been rock climbing for 38 years. Let me use a climbing example to make a point about resting in the spirit. *This truth is vital to living in the New Covenant fully.*

Picture in your mind the scariest mountain face or rock wall you have ever seen. As a rock climber, my task, my dream, my desire, is to surmount this "impossible" goal. It's analogous to the Christian walk.

I might start my rock climbing adventure by purchasing rock climbing books and reading them over and over. But I find when I go out to the rock, I can't make much of the advice and teaching work. So I read and re-read the books again. But the more I try to follow the teaching the more frustrated I become. So, I start attending climbing conferences and seminars even when I can't afford it. I want to learn from the big name speakers who entitle some of their lectures "Seven Keys to Climbing Cracks", and "The Golden Secret of Face Climbing". I attend conference after conference and re-read all my instruction books, yet, I can't apply the ideas and methods well enough to climb this rock wall. I become even more frustrated. What's wrong with me? Maybe I wasn't meant to be a climber? Perhaps I'm supposed to be a simple tourist who stands at the bottom and watches everybody else climb.

Next I obtain a teacher. A master. I travel up to Estes Park, Colorado, and get personal instruction from one of the best in the world – a young man named Tommy Caldwell. He shows me how he does it. I try to imitate Tommy. If this is how Tommy jams his hand into the crack, then I jam my hand exactly the same way. If this is how Tommy jams his climbing shoe into the crack, then that's exactly how I jam my shoe into the crack.

"Just do what the master does," everybody keeps telling me. "Just imitate the master. Climb as he climbs." Sure, sounds real simple. So why doesn't it work?

"Well, maybe you are rebelling against the master without realizing it."

When I hear comments this stupid I really start to wonder about the IQ level of climbers. The more I try to imitate Tommy Caldwell, the more I seem to fail and become deeply discouraged.

The more I fail, the more I want to throw away all my climbing gear and buy a bowling ball! Imitating the master feels like a short cut to burnout. Imitating the master *is* a short cut to burnout!

Tommy has power and strength in a different dimension than I do. As hard as I try, my biceps, forearms and legs only have so much strength and endurance. My attempts to imitate Tommy only leave me feeling like a complete failure. My *desire* and *reality* seem to be growing *apart* – a sure sign burnout is growing within me.

Now . . . what if? What if the very spirit of Tommy Caldwell could enter into my being. What if his spirit filled me and worked with my muscles, my mind and my desires. Tommy's thoughts would become my thoughts. Tommy's power and strength would become my strength. He maintains his personality and I maintain mine. After all, he's Tommy Caldwell and I'm Kim Wenzel!

Now, Tommy starts to climb the rock wall, using my body to climb. That's correct, I become the body of Tommy Caldwell! His spirit guides and directs my every move – *if I let him*. What's my role? How can I allow the spirit of Tommy to empower my muscles, tendons, and ligaments? How can I allow the mind of Tommy to make decisions about which hand hold to use, which foot hold to use? How can I make this work? Simple, but not easy!

I need to stay out of the way, even though I am totally involved! I need to back off, even though I am front and center! I need to surrender myself, even though I am the very package which contains Tommy's spirit! I need to learn how to be totally involved, yet *resting* in Tommy's spirit!

My muscles can now draw on a power and strength beyond themselves. My nerves, ligaments and muscles now work in perfect harmony.

I don't have to worry myself silly about all the safety laws and rules governing climbing – Tommy's spirit is in total harmony with all the rules. I don't have to worry myself silly trying to remember all the principles in the climbing books I have read – Tommy's spirit is the sum total of all the books, methods, principles and techniques.

I no longer need to stress myself out and get headaches trying to decide which hand holds to use. Even this stress can be left up to Tommy. The more I understand this concept, the more I really can *rest* in him. No longer do I have to cry out to Father, "Just tell me which foothold to use! Just tell me, Father! You're the God of love, just give me the answer!" Now . . . I just relax, and let the spirit of Tommy decide which hold to use.

But, if I ever decide to step in and choose a different hand hold than the one Tommy wants to use, his spirit will back off and let me do it my way. This action quickly leads to muscle fatigue and burnout. I start to panic and complain and scream and even start to blame Tommy for the mess I quickly find myself in!

Resting in Tommy's spirit puts me into a situation where my responses to the lead of his spirit can be called faith. Tommy's spirit directs my arm up and jams two fingers in a crack. I look at my situation. I am 1,000 feet off the ground on the rock wall. Tommy's spirit has jammed only two of my fingers into the crack. Fear of falling to my death seems too real to ignore. What do I do? My response to the lead of Tommy's spirit reveals my faith. I either trust Tommy with my life or I don't. Either I believe he knows what he is doing, or I don't. Either he has my best interests at heart or he doesn't. I may choose to step out of resting mode and take matters into my own hands. I direct my entire arm to fit into the crack. Tommy's spirit will allow this. Now I find I cannot move upward or downward! I'm stuck in the crack, rapidly growing tired and frustrated. Tommy's spirit is very kind. He does not laugh at me, or say, "I told you so."

If I never learn to rest in Tommy's spirit, then all my talk about faith is meaningless. The word has no real application when I am not working with Tommy's spirit. My faith is *a response* to his lead. The *rest of faith* occurs when I stay out of the way and enjoy the climb Tommy's doing using my body. *Burnout* is what occurs when I keep stepping in and trying to climb the unclimbable wall myself.

When I learn to *rest* in the very spirit of Tommy Caldwell, I find myself reaching the summit of the mountain. But here is another potential problem of my flesh. I, Kim, stand on the summit, but, it's Tommy who gets all the glory. After all, he is the one who just did the climb – all of it – using my body. Tommy has the right to raise his arms and shout for joy in success. My flesh wars against this. My flesh wants to raise its arms and shout, "*I did it!*"

For my flesh, Tommy getting all the glory is no small pebble along the mountain trail. This is a stumbling stone. In reality, it is the very cornerstone of a successful climb to the summit, but, to the flesh it is a stumbling stone. The spirit of Tommy Caldwell will allow my flesh to take over the climb as many times as need be to where I totally burn out in a heap of exhaustion. I must come to the place where I unconditionally surrender myself and rest.

Here's a hard question. How much of your ministry and walk has been *resting* in the spirit of the Lord Jesus? Answer yourself honestly and it may be the beginning of a whole new chapter of your life!

One of the biggest problems for North American leaders and believers is the John Wayne Syndrome. To rest, and let someone else do it for us is simply un-American. We worship the self-made super-star in business and sports. Even within the North American church we seem to worship the self-made stars whom we look to for answers and direction – even though the Bible says the Holy Spirit is our teacher!

In Chapter 22, we will discuss how "resting in Jesus' spirit" is a short cut to deeper repentance, holiness, character building and having the very mind of Christ – a Tree of Life mind and heart.

NOTES:

NOTES:

NOTES:

Chapter 23

Holiness, Character & the Tree of Life

I have no doubt some will have trouble with the idea of ***resting in the Spirit of Jesus*** as taught in our earlier chapters. The flesh has a real problem with the totally free expression of Father's grace. In fact, our flesh wars against it. We want to do, to achieve, to overcome, to say, "I did it!"

The flesh wars with the spirit, the flesh resents Jesus getting *all* the glory. The flesh wants something to do. The flesh wants some glory, even if it's to say, "I played a role."

Some will say,"Yes, but, what about holiness and building Godly character? Isn't that important? When it comes to salvation, yes, we must trust Jesus, but surely we need to work hard to build character and stay away from the world's bad influence? Shouldn't we be striving to do those things?"

No!

True holiness, not just a form of church culture, should be a product created by allowing the Holy Spirit to flow and do his work in us unhindered. When we rest in the Spirit, as Jesus states in Matt. 11:28-30, we are *getting out of the way* and allowing the one who said he was going to give us a new heart and a renewed mind – do his work. Remember how strong God's statement is in Jer. 31:33-34?

*"This is the covenant **I** will make with the house of Israel*
after that time," declares the LORD.
*"**I** will put my law in their minds*

and write it on their hearts.
***I** will be their God,*
and they will be my people.

34 *No longer will a man teach his neighbor,*
or a man his brother, saying, 'Know the LORD,'
because they will all know me,
from the least of them to the greatest,"
declares the LORD.
*"For **I** will forgive their wickedness*
and will remember their sins no more." (Jer. 31:33-34, NIV)

These wonderful changes are the work of God, not the flesh. Our job or role is to fully cooperate; to get out of the way and allow the Spirit of Jesus to do *His* work. Each time we jump in and do our thing we are slowing down the whole process and creating circumstances that can contribute to burnout. A good example is the very idea of the Tree of Life. After people who have worshiped God in the Tree of Good and Evil learn about the Tree of Life they often get very excited and rush out with the idea of being a Tree of Lifer from that moment on. The more they *try* to live in the Tree of Life, the more they find themselves living and reacting out of the Tree of Good and Evil.

There is only one way to fully jump into the Tree of Life and stay there most of the time. Give up your striving, and let the Spirit take over and guide your life, thoughts, actions and reactions. The Holy Spirit will empower you and inspire you to live in one tree only and that will be the Tree of Life. As the new mind and the new heart are developing inside you under the creative skill of the Holy Spirit, your behavior changes as a *by-product* of your new thinking! It is nothing less than the handiwork of God, not human striving. Holiness is a creative work of God.

Yes, some believers think the changed behavior is Christianity. So they work hard by their own efforts to modify their behavior, and "be Christian." The entire process of the New Covenant is something God is doing. Our role is to cooperate. Remember when Jesus describes our role, He tells us to come to Him, His yoke – the one He lays on us – is *easy*. The burden He gives us is *light* (Matt 11:28-30). Jesus describes it as rest. He wants to give us rest. We don't want rest! We want to do things ourselves, even though we (mankind) proved beyond a shadow of a doubt under the Old Covenant that we can not achieve holiness or righteousness ourselves.

In all areas of holiness and character building, we are speaking of a wonderful work of the Spirit, and our role is to rest in him. I think in many of our conversations we will always speak about such matters as if it were something we are to accomplish, but we need to remember that is not the case. We play our part by surrendering to the Spirit's lead, and these profound changes are God's responsibility.

"But, you're washing away everything that Christianity seems to be. You're watering down everything into a cute cliche' – "rest in the Spirit!"

Please remember Matt. 11:28-30. This is not a cute cliche'. This is the reality of the New Covenant in Jesus' blood. In Gal. 4:4, we are told Jesus came at the *fullness of time*. He came when the religion of the Old Testament had been perverted to its maximum legalism. People were weary and burdened. The New Covenant Jesus was introducing was radically new. It was not just the next covenant in the series. It was new in its very nature.

Previous covenants had been made between God and man. The New Covenant is about God playing the role of both covenant representatives. Father and Jesus. The "newness" of the covenant does not mean *the next one in a series*.

Remember when you were a child, and you received your first tricycle? After mastering it, and growing several inches taller, you started riding a small two wheeler with training wheels. Next, your dad removed the training wheels and you learned balance. Next, your third new cycle was a full size two wheeler. After that, you may have bought for yourself an expensive mountain bike, or perhaps a motorcycle. With each cycle in the series, you proudly announced your “new” cycle to your friends. The cycles were new in the sense that each one was the next in the series.

That does not describe the New Covenant God made with man. This covenant is new in the sense that it is radically different than anything previous. It is not the next one in the series. It stands by itself as a monument to Father’s love for His lost children. *He* is to do it all. *He* makes the covenant – both sides, both representatives. *He* puts the new mind in us. *He* puts the new heart in us. *He* writes *His* laws on our heart. *He* is our God. *He* is our King. *He* is responsible to finish the faith *He* started in us. Praise God!

When we read Jer. 31:33-34 and contemplate the sacrifice of Jesus on the cross, we begin to see the New Covenant is all about God approaching us and saying, "Look my children, what ***I*** have done for you!" The New Covenant has nothing to do with how we can please or impress Him so that He will bless us. The New Covenant has nothing to do with our performance, hair style, worship style or warm smile. The New Covenant is all about the redeeming work of Jesus in saving mankind. The reason Jesus gets the glory is because Jesus does it all!

To rest in the Spirit is anything but a cliche'. It is a bold act of faith. When life crashes down around us and we feel the need to act or react, resting in the Spirit and placing all of our trust in Him is one of the challenges of this life. Cliche'? Not a chance.

NOTES:

NOTES:

NOTES:

Chapter 24

What Freedom Really Is?

Paul, the former legalist, makes a powerful statement in Galatians 5:1. "*It is for freedom that Christ has set us free*." For more than thirty years in the body of Christ I have wondered how many of us really understand freedom? Do we see freedom the same way Father or Jesus does? Can we even understand freedom as well as a former super-legalist such as Paul?

I was born and raised (never reared) in Canada where the government loves to micro-manage people's lives. In some parts of Canada, such as the old British strongholds you need a permit to do anything – blow your nose perhaps! Now that I live in America with my American wife and four American daughters, I can't help notice more freedoms slowly disappearing as elected officials try to manage growing populations and the expenses that come with it. I personally don't think the USA is much behind Canada in over-managing people's lives and choices.

So many in North American churches feel something called ***obligation***. It is an interesting word that reaches inside a person's heart and helps make them do things they might not normally do. To that end, this state called *obligation* carries with it a burden that turns on us like an angry dog and bites us with guilt when we decide to take it easy tonight instead of attending one of a hundred different church functions. Some of these burdens, these yokes, these endless activities that seem to define church life, carry with them these moral commitments that we "do something."

Participate. Help out. Show up. Show your support. Be a doer, not a hearer only! Many people are attracted to church with promises of freedom and rest, and after they are indoctrinated into the congregation the requirements and commitments add up to the point the new member is glad it is Monday morning so they can get back to work and get some rest!

God allowed mankind to learn through the Old Covenant that man is not capable of salvation. We are not capable of deep spiritual healing, Godly character or righteousness apart from God. Here in North America we still like the idea of doing great things by our own wits and strength. So even in our Christianity we still incorporate dozens of obligations which we sometimes teach more vigorously than we teach grace, faith and the Kingdom. So, just what is this freedom that Father values so highly he allowed his son to die on a cross so you and I could have freedom again?

Father values freedom and free choice so much, he refused to show up prematurely in the garden when the serpent was telling lies to the first people. Now, could you do that, or would you need to interfere and give *direction* and *instruction* to the two people?

The freedom Father gives us through Jesus' sacrifice is freedom from sin and self. In a self-help society where only the super-star successes are worshipped, to be free of sin and self is to live in a new dimension from the rest of the human race.

Self, automatically means you. You can do it. You should do it. Why didn't you do it? Strive. Push. Grunt, labor, make it happen. Tremendous stress is placed upon ourselves to achieve. We become driven, and shortly thereafter, disillusioned with life, church and even God – who never told us to strive and drive ourselves into the ground in the first place.

The whole point of the Old Covenant was to prove something to us – but we never listen. The law – striving for obedience and performance – was to be a school teacher to lead us to ***Christ***. We can't do it! God can do it. We are free from a whole lot of self focus, and we are free of the sin that held us in bondage.

We can't do it! Did you hear me? Do you believe it, however? Some of you don't. You still have too much pride of life, but don't worry, if you are reading this book, Father is removing that pride one painful step at a time.

I am now free of religion. I am free of endless man-made rules and traditions. I am free from striving to appease my heavenly Father so he will bless me. I am free of driving myself to some desired goal that defines some form of success. Now, I can relax in Jesus. He is in me and I am in him. Our spirits can flow with love and life back and forth. I can rest in him instead of striving to find him. I can take my hands off the steering wheel and let the Holy Spirit do the steering. I don't have to impress anybody. I don't have to please anybody. I am not caught up in endless ritual and tradition that I am being constantly judged for.

I learn to relax, and let the Holy Spirit do his thing – create a new mind and heart in me. He can do what I never could. I admit I can do nothing apart from Jesus, and that takes incredible pressure off of me. All I do now is walk through life and give away covenant love and life flow from Jesus. I already measure up. Every time Father looks at me, all he sees is the righteousness of Jesus. There is no pressure on me to perform. Jesus already performed to perfection. As Jesus pours covenant love and life into me, I just give it away to everyone around me, and the Kingdom spreads and spreads.

There are no obligations! I don't feel obligated to give away love and life flow from my spirit to another's spirit. It just happens. I love Jesus so much, when he loves me, I just love him and others back again. It becomes an easy natural thing that is so much a part of my new mind and heart and healed spirit that it just happens. Speaking life, and covenant love to others is as natural as breathing. What an easy yoke! What a light burden! Oh, what glorious freedom from religion in Jesus the Christ!

NOTES:

NOTES:

NOTES:

Chapter 25

Introduction to the Sermon on the Mount

When we look at the way Jesus conducted his ministry and relationships, we see the tree of life in action. Despite all the preparation on Father's part to introduce His son and the New Covenant as a radical change from performance based religion, many simply didn't understand. The ideology of needing to please and appease God dated back to the garden. The idea of a God creating a covenant where He did everything, and *imposed* His love and grace upon us to the point our sins are forgiven and a new heart and mind are created within us – well, that's simply too hard to believe for many followers!

In the Sermon on the Mount, Jesus teaches the tree of life approach to living in the New Covenant. For those who live a blend of old and new covenants, some of Jesus' teaching in Matthew 5 through 7 seem extreme. "Jesus exaggerates for emphasis, perhaps," they think. When you understand the nature of the new covenant, and tree of life thinking, suddenly, the Sermon on the Mount becomes clear and a wonderful teaching that makes perfect sense.

Jesus begins by explaining the overall attitude of the tree of life believer. The Beatitudes are one way of capturing this life-giving heart and spirit in words. Jesus' explanation is simple, yet far reaching and profound. People who have never understood the tree of life concept have taught many good sermons on the Beatitudes without fully grasping where Jesus was going with His teaching. In the remainder of Matthew 5, Jesus deals with the dynamics of law and the tree of life.

In Matthew 6, Jesus shows us how easily the flesh creeps into our Christianity, and how we wish to have even a tiny bit of glory for ourselves. In the tree of life we give all glory to God. In the latter part of the chapter the issue of security is dealt with, and the news is exciting and liberating for the tree of lifer.

Relating to others, comparing fruits and building foundations from either tree are covered by Jesus in Matthew 7.

The next three chapters will be dedicated to exploring the Sermon on the Mount in greater detail. I believe living in the tree of life opens the door to continual deepening understanding of truth, and I certainly don't believe my explanation of Matthew 5 through 7 is the final end all of truth. Once you live in the tree of life you can read through the Sermon on the Mount and learn something new each time. May the Lord open your mind and heart while you read the next three chapters! God bless you!

NOTES:

NOTES:

NOTES:

Chapter 26

The Beatitudes

***"Blessed are the poor in spirit, for theirs is the kingdom of heaven. Blessed are those who mourn, for they shall be comforted. Blessed are the meek, for they shall inherit the earth."* (Matthew 5:3-5, NKJV)**

Like many teachings, when people first hear about the tree of life, they want to rush out there into the world and speak life to everyone everywhere. The world can be a tough place, and before they realize it, these well intentioned believers have slipped back into tree of good and evil thinking and reacting.

So, how do we stay in the tree of life with any consistency? What is the state of our being that helps us stay focused on life, and giving life away to others? Part of the answer is in the first three beatitudes Jesus taught. Being poor in spirit, mourning, and meekness. In our modern language we can call these three attitudes or states of spirit – humble, broken and teachable.

God gives grace to the humble. Jesus, Himself, displayed humility for all generations to follow. When we are deeply humble, our focus is God, not self. Worship becomes a major activity in our lives. We give Him *all* the glory, so the focus is automatically upon Him. It isn't something we need to remember. It is a natural part of our daily lives.

When self becomes the focus, doing things for self and to exalt self are natural. So brokenness and humility are twins, each helping the other. God gets a real charge out of people who are of a broken and contrite spirit, and tremble at His word (Isa.66:2). Why? It takes profound brokenness to stop, and simply rest in Jesus' spirit. When we are at our weakest, the Holy Spirit can really do His thing in and through us.

If we are not meek, that is, not teachable, how can we allow the Holy Spirit to do the leading? How can we rest in His spirit and let Him handle the situation, when we already know everything? Deep humility, total brokenness and a yielding teachable spirit allows us to give the Holy Spirit freedom to carry out the dynamics of the New Covenant. Without these three states of spirit and heart, resting in the spirit and living in the tree of life are impossible.

When our self will is completely crucified the door opens for the Holy Spirit to build the new mind and heart in us. As that mind and heart develop, staying in the tree of life and resting in Jesus'spirit become normal behavior.

When deep humility becomes an anchor in our spirit, then ours is the kingdom of heaven. That is, we are walking the kingdom walk on the earth, and being the salt of the earth. When we are humble enough to rest in Jesus' spirit and live in the tree of life, we are no longer humans having a spiritual experience, but spirits having a human experience.

When you have mourned deep in your own brokenness and have been comforted by God, you then can reach out to others who are mourning and speak blood covenant love into their spirits. We then become comfort agents to this hurting world. What better way to heal than to speak life and healing into others who are like sheep without a shepherd!

"Blessed are those who hunger and thirst for righteousness, for they shall be filled." (verse 6, NKJV)

Jesus shows us, once we are broken to the point of deep humility and a teachable spirit, many of the earthly hungers we have will be replaced by a spiritual one – hunger for righteousness. When we rest in His spirit and let the Holy Spirit do the driving, a greater appetite for the things of God develops. The more we hunger for the flow of the Holy Spirit, the more He will do and the greater the flow of Covenant love and God life in us. We will be filled! But it all starts with humility, brokenness and a teachable spirit.

Jesus gives a planned approach. First he lays out the inner state of being that we need – humility, brokenness and teachability. Then, he launches into what would become our *new* natural hunger, righteousness and things of the spirit. Next Jesus introduces the characteristics of our new life as a spirit having a human experience – displaying mercy to a lost world, thinking in a pure manner, and introducing a whole new way to make peace.

"***Blessed are the merciful, for they shall obtain mercy. Blessed are the pure in heart, for they shall see God. Blessed are the peacemakers, for they shall be called the sons of God.*** (verses 7-9, NKJV)

Picture in your mind a profoundly humble believer going through life, knowing the power within him; knowing the power of speaking life to a lost wounded soul. Knowing the power that would flow from him to the wounded – the power of blood covenant love! As Jesus speaks to his disciples on the hillside, he can see it all in his mind's eye. Father's children, spiritual beings in a human experience, letting mercy flow out of them to hurting humans having a hellish experience on this earth. As the believers sow to the spirit, of the spirit they reap. The believer speaks life and mercy into the hurting soul of another, and life and covenant love flows from God to the believer. The flow of Father's love is without end. The more we give away to others, the more Father gives us. By speaking mercy and life into the hurting, we ourselves become overflowing with what we give away!

This power flow in turn helps purify our motives. We see the power and the work we have here on the earth in a new light. We stop focusing on our own pain and lack, and begin to be conduits of Father's love and life to others. The pure heart is created within us by the Holy Spirit.

Mankind makes peace by killing off his enemy. Jesus tells us if we live by the sword, we die by the sword. Several thousand years of human history on planet earth confirm Jesus' words. So, what is a peacemaker in Jesus' eyes? Peacemaking can take many forms, but let's review what we have said in the theme of this book.

Abigail spoke life and peace into David's spirit. David spoke life and peace into Mephibosheth's spirit. Jesus spoke peace and forgiveness into the spirit of many sinners of his day. When a believer is humble, broken and teachable, walking in the flow of blood covenant love and life, they have within them more power than an M16 rifle. More power than a cruise missile, more power than a B1 bomber! It is the power of Father's blood covenant love. The power to change a spirit. The flesh may still be cursing you to your face, but if you keep speaking life and love into the enemy's spirit, they will blink. They may even become a good friend someday. Jesus tells us we can truly be called sons of God when we practice this approach to peacemaking.

"Blessed are those who are persecuted for righteousness' sake, for theirs is the kingdom of heaven. Blessed are you when they revile and persecute you, and say all kinds of evil against you falsely for My sake.<verses 10-11, NKJV)

In a negative cynical world, if you walk around speaking life into everyone, and have a positive optimistic viewpoint, there will be some who find you a threat. Your love and visible life flow will be offensive to their preference of living in victimization. Your life-giving spirit takes the wind out of their dooms-day sails. Your positive opinion of peoples' futures takes away the gossip's secret ingredient. Your flow of covenant love to the weak offends their enemies. Your simple faith and trust in Jesus to help you out of tragedy insults the complainer's pride.

In short, as a spirit walking in the spirit and having a human experience on this earth, you just don't fit in, dude! The world is full of humans struggling in a hellishly selfish existence, using escapism as a means of coping with pain and hopelessness. You are a new creation from some other place (where did you say your citizenship was from?). You bring an attitude, a life and a flow of love that comes from another dimension. As we used to say back in the 60's, "you're way out, dude." No wonder tree of lifers are persecuted for Jesus' sake!

NOTES:

NOTES:

NOTES:

Chapter 27

The Tree of Life in Matthew 5

Salt and Light
verses 13-16

If salt loses it's flavor, how shall it be seasoned? If, as believers, we walk around with no blood covenant love and God-life flowing out of us, what good are we as New Covenant representatives? What makes a New Covenant believer so radically different than any other religious person is that *life flow* and *love flow* that impacts the very spirits of those we come in contact with. If those two powerful elements are not pouring out of us, we will be like many other religious people – mean, judgmental, and hard to be around.

When blood covenant *love* and *life* are flowing freely, it is like a light that shines everywhere. You can't hide it anymore than you can a hilltop city. This life flow is to profoundly impact others so they will give glory to our heavenly Father.

Law and Prophets
verses 17-20

In introducing the New Covenant Tree of Life approach, Jesus did not come to destroy the law or the prophets. The prophets testified of Jesus and the new covenant he would bring in his blood, and the law was to be our school master to show us we simply could never, ever, achieve holiness and righteousness on our own. The law and prophets underscore our need for a whole new relationship basis with God. Performing and appeasing God to get a blessing is no longer the name of the game. The eternal life-giving principles behind the law will always be, but now we can go well beyond mere obedience into spirit communion with Father's spirit. Life and covenant love can flow from His spirit to ours, and back again, as well as out to other people – even our enemies. As with any blood covenant, the greater king imposes the conditions of covenant upon the lesser king. In this case, Father is imposing His love and grace upon his children who are incapable of holiness by performance. The Pharisees represent performance mode, and the tree of life believer is to have righteousness that surpasses that approach. The tree of lifer has a new heart and mind and healed spirit created by the Father's flow of life and covenant love!

Murder and Adultery
verses 21-28

Jesus now jumps into specific examples. Under the old way of thinking, as long as you didn't murder your enemy you were fine. You could secretly hate his guts if you liked. In hatred, however, we have a different flow between spirits. We have the flow of death. Hatred and murder take us in the same direction. God moves in the direction we call life. When hatred exists in the spirit of a believer, it cuts off or slows the flow of life and covenant love. Jesus feels so strong on this point, he tells us to leave our gift for God at the altar, go and get the spirit of death out of our heart regarding our enemy, and then come back to the alter to freely accept the flow of life and love from God. However we need to work it out with our adversary, we need to do it quickly. The best way is to speak love and life into the adversary, and win him over as a friend if possible. By speaking life and love to another we are certainly opening the flow of love from Father. The same principles apply to the subject of adultery. Even if our body isn't moving toward death, our imagination may be. The end result is still death. Jump back into life! Jesus tells us vividly that death needs to be cut off. He uses such imagery as plucking out your eye, and cutting off your hand. Death's direction in us must die, so covenant love and life can flow.

Divorce and Oaths
verses 31-37

Why does God hate divorce? Several reasons. One very good reason is because divorce is a type of death. Marriage is a communion of three spirits; husband, wife and Jesus the Christ. A great marriage is when life and love flow freely between all three spirits. When divorce happens, life and love stop flowing, and are often replaced with death and bitterness. A divinely ordained covenant of love flow is broken. We have already noted that speaking life into another's spirit can change the other's whole approach to life. Many marriages can be saved by speaking life into our mate even when our mate shows nothing but hatred for us. When divorce is chosen, we are allowing the end of spirit communion and the flow of death continues.

With our speech, we need to let our yes be yes, and our no be no. There is life and death in the power of the tongue. When we start to speak all kinds of promises and grandiose commitments to others, we are setting up their hearts for expectations. Unfulfilled expectations are one of the greatest sources of hurt and wounding of a person's spirit. A tree of lifer walking in the New Covenant is in the business of healing wounded spirits and breathing life into those wounded spirits. To create even a hint of death in another is to do great harm. We should all be slow to speak, long on listening, and when we do speak, let it be life!

Eye for an Eye
verses 38-48

Just how totally radical is this tree of life approach to walking in the New Covenant in Jesus blood? The final ten verses of chapter five can disturb even aging veterans of the body of Christ. Here Jesus lays out what seems to be advice that is totally contrary to common sense.

When someone slaps us on the cheek, the natural reaction is to clench our fist, pull back our arm and knock out their front teeth! Naturally, this causes the person with no front teeth to clench their fist and knock out our front teeth. After a while the only clear winner is the local dentist who can now afford a new set of golf clubs.

What Jesus is teaching us at the end of chapter five is to stop the flow of death as quickly as possible, even if there is a cost to us that seems unfair or unjust. That unfair price is a small price to pay if it keeps you moving toward life – because Jesus is LIFE. So, we turn the other cheek. We don't give our enemy any reason to continue the attack against us. Our flesh does not like the price we pay however. It is exactly during these moments in life we find out how much we are led by the spirit of Jesus and how much by our own human spirit and nature. It can be discouraging!

When a Roman soldier commands us to carry his pack a mile, we willingly choose to carry the burden two miles. It gives us more time to pray for the soldier and his family. We have more time to speak life into his spirit and perhaps be a tool in the hands of the master carpenter who may be working out a miracle in the soldier's heart.

When we are cursed, we return the comments with blessings upon the enemy with life and love. We do good things for people who hate us. We pray for people who spitefully use us and persecute us. Why? Two reasons.

First, these reactions inside us stop the flow of death in our heart, stone cold.

Second, speaking life into the enemy's heart causes life and love to flow in us as well as our enemy, who may someday be a friend! When there is death in our heart and spirit, the flow of Father's love and life is halted. By breathing life into an enemy we are assuring Father's love will flow in us and our adversary.

Anybody can love their best friend. You need the flow of God's love in your being to love your enemy. So this tree of life walk with Jesus is totally impossible to hide. Loving your enemies makes your light shine like a city on top a hill. You become the salt of society, making everyone thirsty for covenant love and the free flow of life that seems to turn the world up side down. Your whole focus now becomes glorifying Father through giving away life and love to the lost who need it desperately. No longer are you preoccupied with yourself, your problems, your sins, your need to overcome, your performance. While you are busy glorifying Father by imparting life and love to the hurting, the Holy Spirit is creating a new mind and a new heart in you! So, in the end, we end up perfect (mature) like our heavenly Father! (Verses 48)

NOTES:

NOTES:

NOTES:

Chapter 28

The Tree of Life in Matthew 6

Charitable Deeds before Men
verses 1-4

Performance based religion has many disguises. When we are not busy impressing and appeasing God, we are striving to impress our fellow believers. The selfish will does not want to die, yet God life will not flow freely when selfishness is parading itself about. To allow for the greatest amount of love and life flow in our spirits, we must remember to keep the self-will buried at the bottom of the baptism tank. Again, Jesus is telling us to stop the flow of death, stone cold!

When self-will is thwarted, a new expression of death often reigns as we express our frustration and anger. The flow of death has as many disguises as our self-will.

The remedy: Don't let your left hand know what your right hand is doing. Simply put, never, never, never look for any throne of importance or recognition from mankind. Like Jonathan coming before David, constantly remind Jesus He is the King and we renounce any claim of any credit or importance. We just want to be princes and princesses at His right hand side.

When You Pray
verses 5-8

The same selfish principles can apply to prayer also. Many want to be seen or have a reputation as a super-star prayer warrior. Some seem to believe if they shout loud in public prayer that is a sure sign of fervency, or perhaps God, who is hard of hearing, will hear them better should they scream and demand in an authoritarian voice.

By this point in the book I hope we all see that any sign of selfishness, or self-exaltation is a door way to the spirit of death. When all the human nature in us stays dead in the bottom of the baptismal, and we are vessels of Father's will, the blood covenant love and life of Jesus is free to flow like a mighty river. Let us avoid drawing attention to ourselves, and allow the salt and light of the covenant draw all attention to God.

Life-Giving Prayer
verses 9-13

In the example prayer Jesus gave us, we are speaking life and profound worship to our Father. It is His name, not ours, that we are hallowing and glorifying. It is His Kingdom, not ours, we are praising and desiring to manifest. It is His will, not ours, we wish to see expressed in every activity we are involved in. The same basic principle of speaking life into another spirit will create a return flow of life certainly applies with God. The more we honor Him and speak life to Him, the more His life flows into and out of us!

We ask him to forgive us in the same degree that we have forgiven others, and so we acknowledge the criteria for the flow of life and covenant love. If we live in death by refusing to forgive those who have hurt us, how can the free flow of love and life come to us from Father? No, we must keep the flow way wide open with love, life and forgiveness to others pouring out of us, and then the flow from Father to us is unimpeded. But, even in this, the grace of God is there to help us, since forgiving another can be a great obstacle.

When we ask for help in avoiding temptation, we are attempting to head off the spirit of death at the pass, before it even has a chance to enter our lives. We are saying pro-actively that we desire today to walk in life, and stay in life.

Forgiveness – the Door to Life-Flow
verses 14-15

In these two verses, Jesus states so clearly the spiritual principle again. If only death flows between us and others, the very spirit of Father's life can not and will not reside in us. If we are walking, thinking and talking death – we are headed in the opposite direction from Father, thus it becomes impossible to be fully forgiven by Him because He and His family are moving into life, not death. We can not be with God and moving in the opposite direction from God at the same time. Forgiveness – toward others and self – needs to be a mind set, a normal attitude and approach in our relationships throughout life. When it is, the world knows us for the love we have for one another. When forgiveness isn't the mindset of the believer, the world knows us for two basic characteristics. Meanness, and self-righteousness.

Fasting – Motive
Verses 16-18

It would seem, even in our efforts to draw near to Jesus, a selfish motive can enter the equation. Any time we think we can do something to please or impress Father, with a motive behind it to get Father to do something for us – we are moving in death. God is sovereign, and always knows best. Our control and manipulation techniques for selfish gain do not promote life in Father or ourselves. It's simply a power play for selfish ends. When church members do this to their pastor, he certainly doesn't find it life-giving. Neither does our heavenly Father.

Keep this simple fact in mind. Life flows in the purist of motives, but death starts to creep in with any selfishness on our part.

Treasure in Heaven
Verses 19-24

Do not. When we read these verses do we really read that phrase – "do not?" Do not store up treasures on earth – but isn't that what I see so many believers doing in America today? Where ever we store up treasure is where our heart is – earth, or heaven. If you desire the earthy treasure, you will often slide into a very different mentality than we find in the tree of life. The attitude in the tree of life is one of giving away. Giving life, hope, encouragement, and what ever else God has gifted us in. When it comes to any kind of earthly treasure there are two factors to keep in mind.

(1) How do I accumulate this treasure? By what means and methods?

(2) How do I prevent the loss and destruction of this treasure by all the forces active in this life?

That is a very different direction of thought and preoccupation than the tree of life, which is constantly asking, how can I breathe life into this person or situation. It is the constant giving away of God life and God love to others. Tree of life living is the philosophy of, "What's mine is yours." And what's mine has become so much more than money, extra clothing, temporary shelter, and extra meals to the hungry. We now *have* and can give away *blood covenant love and the flow of real life* from Father.

The other two philosophies of living, "What's yours is mine," and, "What's mine is mine," are involved in accumulating. Not just money, but treasures like power, influence, fame, control, notoriety, with the subtle and sometimes not so subtle purpose of self-promotion. The Priest and Levite on the road to Jericho were far more concerned with themselves and "their" ministry to give away life to the bleeding man on the side of the road.

Do Not Worry!
Verses 25-34

So, if you choose to walk in life, and practice the philosophy, "What's mine is yours," how do we deal with the pulls of the other two life philosophies? We can't serve God and money, but we all need money while we walk this earth. So . . . if I spend my life giving away life and covenant love in all it's forms and ways, will Father see me through? Can I really walk in this wonderful philosophy?

Jesus states clearly, in black and white, we are not to worry about food and clothing. In black and white terms Jesus says the pagans worry about such things. We are not pagans, but servants of Jesus, ambassadors charged with giving away love and life to the lost. He tells us so clearly that Father knows what we already need! But do we really trust Him that much?

Our role? First, we are to seek the Kingdom and Jesus' righteousness. Seeking the Kingdom first isn't just reading the Bible and praying every morning. It is also all about the giving away of life, mercy, grace, and hope to those who need it. When we do these things Jesus promises the Father will give to us all the things we need like food and clothing.

So Jesus ends this teaching with his patent conclusion, "Therefore." Therefore, do not worry about tomorrow, for tomorrow will worry about itself. Each day has enough trouble of its own.(verse 34).

How many of us in modern America can live by that last statement? My guess is extremely few. In many of our churches we preach so much humanism, we actually teach the opposite of the truth Jesus gave us. We teach people to trust human planning and methodology, schemes, long term goal setting – as if we could control and manage our lives. How quickly we forget we died in the waters of baptism, and now we are not to even worry about tomorrow! ***Tomorrow!*** Surely Jesus didn't really mean that, did he?

This is tough teaching for people who live by one of the first two philosophies of life. When you are climbing your own ladder and building your own kingdom, the teachings of Jesus are very hard indeed. When you are in a continuous state of giving away – so much is flowing into you from Father, you don't need to worry about tomorrow!

We may plan past tomorrow, but we are told to never forget an important element in our planning – the statement – "God willing."

NOTES:

NOTES:

NOTES:

Chapter 29

The Tree of Life in Matthew 7

Do Not Judge
Verses 1-2

Here, Jesus is teaching very clearly about thinking, our thought processes. We are constantly making evaluations throughout the day, regarding ten thousand different topics. Jesus isn't against evaluating, but is against judging – that is a type of condemnation of others.

In the work place you may evaluate two people and promote one of them. When we get into condemnation and gossip we are thinking and speaking death. Jesus' teaching on that direction of thinking is clear – DO NOT! We need to stay in life, and promote life when ever possible. If we get into speaking death to some people, the same measure often comes back to us. We are to rise above that, and promote life in every way.

Speck of Sawdust
Verses 3-5

Why do we so very easily see the speck of sawdust in another's eye, and not our own? Simply because that direction of thinking is tree of the knowledge of good and evil. Remember the world-view of a person living in the tree of death? Because they now know good from evil they are preoccupied with right and wrong. They "See, Know, Judge, Condemn," and thus, what is wrong with another stands out like the Grand Canyon. Even if it is just a speck of sawdust, they can see it from 50 feet away.

Jesus tells us so clearly that is hypocrisy. We all have dust in our eyes and cannot see reality properly. First, we need to have that deeply broken and contrite spirit that allows us to live in the tree of life, then we will be able to help our friend. We will be more than willing to speak life into their lives to the point they start to see clearly also! Praise Jesus!

Dogs, Pearls and Pigs
Verse 6

In this life there are forces of death everywhere. Although we always want to respond to death with the power of life, we need to use wisdom. Some agents of death will simply trample our encouragement, love and grace shown to them. Don't allow this to discourage you. In the ultimate end, life is more powerful than death. Be wise in dealing with people in the work place, and even in the church. Some can be shown the pearls of Jesus' love, others are tares sown in with the wheat and they may trample your efforts to help them.

Ask, Knock, Seek
Verses 7-12

Ask, knock, seek! Awesome! So, where's my new BMW?

Uh, read verse 12 first.

"So, in everything, do to others what you would have them do to you, for this sums up the Law and the Prophets." (NIV) This section of teaching has to do with relating to others. Jesus is continuing on from the pigs trampling the pearls. The correct way to relate is to treat others as you would want to be treated: respectfully, gracefully, with

proper honor. When it comes to cracking the hard nut, we can ask, seek, knock, and find a way to speak life and covenant love into the heart of another.

Father will give us gifts to reach out and give away the truth to others we meet.

Narrow Gate, Wide Gate
Verses 13-14

The wide gate is so well traveled. The wide gate is everywhere, including our TV sets, and magazines. The tree of life, the narrow gate, is one not as well understood as it should be. The tree of life is free of religion, and full of relationship; the communion of Jesus' spirit with our spirit. The narrow gate is the flow of life and covenant love between spirits – that leads all of us into greater love and relationship with the King of Kings.

Tree and Fruit
Verses 15-23

Why do we need to beware of false prophets? Very simple. They operate out of the wide gate (tree of death) and appeal to your selfishness. By their fruit you will know them. Do they focus your eyes on the Kingdom, or on one of your personal needs or wants? Do they focus your eyes on heaven or on earthly desires of success? Do they teach you how to give, give, give away life and covenant love, or on how to have and obtain?

A tree (or gate) is know by it's fruits. If it is the tree of the knowledge of good and evil, you will sooner or later become very disillusioned with church and religion. If it is the tree of life, you will become more alive than you have been before and start to give away the life and love of Christ. There will be the flow of life and love between spirits.

How important is this flow of life and love between your spirit and Jesus' spirit? Well, verses 21-23 are shocking. You may know about Jesus intellectually and do some wonderful works in his name, but if there has been no flow of life and covenant love between you and him, he just might say, "I never *knew* you. Away from me, you evildoers."

The narrow gate is not religion. It is a living, dynamic relationship with our King, where life and love flow like rivers back and forth between him and us, and between each other.

Foundations
Verses 24-27

When life is good, we are not always aware of which tree we live in. When the winds and storms of life come our way, we often find out what our foundation really is. Any house looks good on a calm sunny day, but let a hurricane blow in and many find their heart is still in the tree of good and evil. Base your life on LIFE and covenant love, and you can withstand any storm.

One Who Had Authority
Verses 28-29

The teachers of the law had a very academic, intellectual approach. And it did little to inspire and motivate people. Jesus came along and spoke life and allowed covenant love to flow out of him into the wounded spirits of his day, and people became excited and moved to walk with God. For the first time, people had a reason to draw near to God.

NOTES:

NOTES:

NOTES:

Chapter 30

The Tree of Life in Matthew 8

If you are Willing?
Verses 1-4

When Jesus starts down the mountainside, the first person he comes to is a person totally rejected by society – a leper. The man is slowly dying of his skin disease, and he seeks out LIFE to heal him. Jesus' statement to the man's question is simple, and powerful.

"I am willing, be clean." First however, Jesus reached out his hand and touched the leper. I am sure there were gasps among the gathered. One thing a good clean citizen never does is touch a leper! Yet, the servant of God, with the mission to introduce people to life, real life, reaches out and touches the untouchable.

Are we willing? The Priest and the Levite on the road to Jericho didn't want blood and dirt on their hands. They kept right on trucking, they had "important" ministry to carry out!

In those simple words, "I am willing," there is hope for mankind. Even if we are in a state of total rejection from our fellow man, the King of Kings is willing to pour out blood covenant love and life to us.

Centurion Faith
Verses 5-13

The centurion needed the flow of life for his servant. Life flows in different ways, sometimes in healing the physical body. The centurion understands life flows from Father to us in the same manner authority flows and has a power to make things happen. Do we believe it? Do you comprehend a real flow of life and love or is this strictly academic? When the woman with the 12 year flow touched Jesus' hem, life and love flowed out of him and he perceived it. She was healed by the flow.

We can see from these verses some Kingdom subjects really don't believe these truths, and they will be thrown out into outer darkness.

In verses 14-17, we see life and love flowing again in the form of healing. Jesus loves giving away life and covenant love to those in need.

Cost of Following Jesus
Verses 18-22

When the one fellow said, "Teacher, I will follow you wherever you go," is it possible there was a selfish motive in his heart? Could his human nature have been climbing a ladder to get in good with the master? It is possible.

Jesus explains with absolute clarity that this walk he is on is one of selfless giving away, and not the acquiring of anything. "Foxes have holes and birds of the air have nests, but the Son of Man has no place to lay his head." If we are to follow him, realize the giving away of covenant love, grace, mercy, time, energy, healing, food, forgiveness, life itself, is what this New Covenant/New Way of the Spirit is all about. If you plan or hope to gain anything from it, you are mistaken. You are an Ambassador of Christ – an agent – with the purpose of giving away Kingdom life and Covenant love. Forget yourself, and what you want.

The next fellow in line to proclaim dedication to Jesus wanted to go home first and bury his human father who had just died; a normal part of life on this planet. But, notice Jesus' response!

"Follow me, and let the dead (spiritually) bury their own dead (physically dead)." It would seem Jesus was so tuned into giving away life he made this comment. We all attend to the dead when it comes time for a funeral. In fact some families only get together when someone gets married or buried. The rest of our lives we may have nothing to do with siblings scattered across the globe. Why? We are very tuned into our own life, desires and immediate family.

Jesus and the tree of life are so different that most believers just don't get it. We should use every opportunity to let life flow to everyone we can!

Wind and Waves, Life and Death
Verses 23-27

Why does a furious storm come up as soon as Jesus and the men climb into the boat? Anytime, any place the enemy can try to snuff out the flow of life, he will try. He no longer has the legal right to do so, but he always tries.

If the forces of death can create wind and waves, can the power of life silence the wind and waves? That question opens some interesting doors of thought. Ponder on that for a while.

When the disciples react to the potential of death, Jesus tells them they have little faith. We are in the same boat as the disciples! Jesus, LIFE himself, is always with us, yet we, too, sometimes react with plain old fear to the strategies of the devil. Here is a thought. If Jesus was willing to stand up and rebuke the physical elements with the love and the life he was receiving from Father, should you and I not be willing to stand up and rebuke the physical circumstances that can hold us back from Kingdom work?

Demons, Pigs and Jesus
Verses 28-34

When the flow of life and covenant love come to a place, many things change so dramatically, some folks don't like it. They find it so different they ask LIFE to leave and go somewhere else. This can certainly happen in our ministry and personal lives. Just as speaking life and love caused the biggest sinners in town to love and invite Jesus over for supper repeatedly, the flow of his life and love also turned off this particular community so much, they asked him to leave. It mattered not that two human beings were saved from demon possession. What mattered most to them was the loss of money with the drowning of the pigs. Beware, even in the church today we have people whose god is money, not Jesus.

NOTES:

NOTES:

NOTES:

Chapter 31

Musings on Secular Humanism

or
Why Jesus would Never Read Modern Christian Success Literature

I was standing in the sanctuary of a mega-church a number of years ago, and a fellow former pastor was chatting with me about messages in churches. He asked me a rather simple question.

"When was the last time you heard a sermon on The Kingdom of God?"

I had to ponder his question for I had no instant answer. After a few moments I had to admit it had been so long since I heard a full sermon inspiring me about the future glory of The Kingdom that I could not put a time frame to the answer. Over the last many years I had listened to hundreds of sermons on how to live in the here and now; how to be successful at this or that; how to achieve happiness in this life. Some of these messages were very appealing and seemed "spiritual" in the delivery. But as for reaching inside me and touching my heart with a vision of excitement about eternity – well, I just could not remember when I had heard a sermon that did that in the last ten years.

Our bookstores are filled with religious writings that parallel the sermons we hear. Between the Sunday sermons, the books we read, the tapes and CDs we listen to, we should be the most balanced, super successful believers in the history of the church! Yet . . . most churches are stagnant in grow or in slow decline, and worldwide as many as 16 million people walk out of church each year and never come back – according to the World Christian Encyclopedia.

How well do we see secular humanism in the church? Why are we so focused on the here and now, and rarely get our eyes off the horizon and focus on eternity? Why has formula living taken over the church. We have methods, techniques, recipes, seven step formulas to success in everything – they have become the main stay of church teaching. Our pride is satisfied with all this methodology because this approach gives us some control. We still feel in charge of our life. We kid ourselves by saying we are living our life ***for*** Jesus, when we are supposed to be living our life ***from*** Jesus.

When I traveled the road of Bible university I was bombarded with the idea of goal setting and micro-managing my life. If you don't have a goal, you have no direction, no purpose, and you will not arrive at your destination. You need short term, medium term and long term goals, and a driving, striving determination to get there to succeed. "Never give up on your dreams! Never give up on your goals!" they would preach.

After university, Kathy and I headed out to the field ministry and pastored churches for the next twenty years, and read all kinds of books by big named preachers who preached the same approach to this life; endless goal setting, time management, learning to say no, striving, driving, and relentlessly praying and fasting, not to mention endless management and leadership skills.

The underlying premise of all this "Christian success" approach seemed to say to me, "Kim, it's up to you. You're in charge of your own life and decisions." It all sounded so logical, yet, I always had trouble dovetailing these ideas with scripture.

I thought I died in the baptism tank. Going into that watery grave I died to self and to the world's operating system. If I did, why worry about my goals? It's Father's goals that are now the issue isn't it? I thought my life was one of total and complete brokenness and humility before Father and Jesus, so why is the development of my self-esteem so important? I thought my life was to be defined by Jesus' definition of success, so why do the world's standards of success end up preached so often on Sunday?

When I look at Jesus' life in scripture it seems so very different from mine. Nearly the opposite. I live in a Martha society. Rush here, rush there, get to this meeting or that meeting. Call this person, email that person, read this book, hurry, hurry, hurry.

Jesus lived a Mary life. He had one primary focus – Father God. As Jesus walked from point A to point B with the disciples, a man could run up and say, "Lord, I have a servant sick at my house, can you come and heal him?"

I want you to notice what Jesus **didn't do.** He didn't look at his watch! He didn't hum and haw and tell the guy he was booked up for the next several days. He didn't tell the fellow to call his secretary to make an appointment. He didn't mutter to himself about this interruption playing havoc with his short term goals.

Jesus' attitude was, "Sure, let's go." It was an opportunity to do good. To speak life into a sick person, and share some covenant love with others. It was an opportunity to show off a Tree of Life approach in a lost society. It was ***not*** an interruption that slowed Jesus down in achieving His dreams. It was a divine opportunity for the Father to achieve His dreams, through Jesus!

Jesus was not troubled by time. He often stopped to talk, tell stories, or pray for someone. He had time to climb a mountain before a teaching session, or sail across the sea. When invited to a long evening of dinner and storytelling, he always had the time. Jesus did not come across purpose driven, but rather, *spirit-led.*

I love the way Pastor Mark Buchanan sums up Jesus' days in his book, The Rest of God. *"His days, as far as we can figure, were a series of zig-zags and detours, off-the-cuff plans, spur-of-the-moment decisions, leisurely meals, serendipitous rounds of storytelling."*

Here in driven American we would call that life-style *retirement*! At Smoldering Wick Ministries we call it, "resting in the spirit." In the Bible it is called the "new way of the spirit."

Here is a very non-purpose driven way of describing Jesus' walk through a day – from John 3:8

"The wind blows where ever it pleases. You hear its sound, but you can not tell where it comes from or where it is going. ***So is everyone born of the Spirit****."*(emphasis mine).

Jesus had a different approach than all of us type A personalities. Acts 10:38 sums it up nicely in Peter's words, *"God anointed Jesus of Nazareth with the Holy Spirit and power, and he went around doing good and healing all who were under the power of the devil, because God was with him."*

He went around doing good. He didn't go around fulfilling his endless goal list. He didn't go around seeking his own peace of mind or personal blessing. He just went around doing good; Speaking life, sharing covenant love, and healing people under the devil's influence. Jesus' focus was not his own life, goals, dreams, hopes, or ambitions. Everything Jesus did was because he heard the Father speak it first. Jesus was precisely tuned into the Father's desires and goals, not his own. Jesus gained his life and purpose by losing it to the Father's will – *"not my will, but yours be done."*

I never stop being amazed how many believers still think they are in charge of their own lives. It is as if we want both Father's dream, and the American Dream all rolled into one nice neat package. If you are a believer, ask yourself if you truly died in the waters of baptism (Romans 6).

If so, don't talk about your ministry, your life, your marriage, your problem, your need, your blessing, your miracle, your anointing, your gifting, your sacrifice, your, your, your, your, your. It's all about Jesus and the Kingdom, not us and our needs and wants.

Yes, Father promises to give us the desires of our heart, but what we forget is our heart is to be the very heart of Jesus. We died in the baptism tank (or sprinkling). The desires Father will fulfill have to do with the lost and with the Kingdom.

When it comes to growing and being successful from a Kingdom standpoint, Father has the perfect plan. It's called life on earth. Look honestly at your experiences. Where have you often grown the most? By fulfilling a personal goal? Or by an interruption that turned your life inside out?

Life isn't easy. Secular humanism masquerading as Christianity can't make it easy or workable! When your teen daughter comes home and says, "Dad, I'm sorry. I'm pregnant," you enter into a stage of dynamic growth few humanly set goals could ever achieve.

Interruptions, trials, unexpected phone calls, people dropping in uninvited – all these and ten million more experiences are ***not interferences*** with your life – *they are your life* – many of them God appointed!

Relax. Learn to rest in the very Spirit of Jesus. He is the author and the finisher of your faith. Do you know what that means? With a book, the author gets it started, but the publisher and editors do the finishing. Not so with Jesus. He is your author *and finisher*. Do you really get that concept? He has prepared a place for you in his eternal government which will expand in every direction for eternity, and now he is preparing you for that position. Nothing is left to chance. Whatever experiences you need to mold and shape you to fit the place, Jesus will allow and even engineer himself to make sure you are ready. Rest in Jesus' Spirit and you will fulfill our Father's goals and dreams. Get out of the Martha lifestyle with all its methods, recipes, books, success CD's, and techniques. Learn to mellow like Mary, and choose the better part.

NOTES:

NOTES:

NOTES:

Chapter 32

FINAL WORD

There is no quick fix for burnout. Father gives us no short cuts, no seven easy steps to healing from deep wounding and rejection. There is only cold hard reality.

Reality Fact: Over the past two thousand years the greatest persecution of believers has come from *inside the church.* Some of God's most powerful tools have been beaten, abused and even put to death by the church.

Reality Fact: God's servants are not promised a rose garden. Here on earth, God's leaders have been misquoted, mistreated, some poverty stricken, some health afflicted, most rejected. Jesus tells his servants they will be hated because he was hated, and they will be persecuted because he was persecuted, and they will enter the Kingdom through *much tribulation.* The high profile mega-church pastor with the Lear jet is anything but the Biblical stereo type.

Reality Fact: The joy of the Lord is your strength. When we finally die to self – I mean really die to self – all our hopes and dreams and ambitions – die to self and totally allow the Holy Spirit to take the steering wheel of our lives – only then can we learn to *rest* in Jesus' Spirit and find joy in the Lord Jesus. Our heavenly Father will allow burnout, disillusionment and depression to come upon us to bring us to this level of brokenness.

Reality Fact: Healing from burnout and deep spiritual wounding comes only from a new revelation of Jesus in our lives. Jesus doesn't give us a fix, he gives us himself, and if we lose ourselves completely in him, we will be deeply healed.

Reality Fact: We, as followers of Christ Jesus, are to be called, chosen and faithful. If you have gone through a burn-out experience it is still part of the process. We may go through twenty years of life in our calling before we realize we are chosen to suffer for Christ's sake. Now is our time of faithfulness. Will we stay faithful? Will we stay the course? Will we allow Jesus to perfect His holiness in us? Will we allow patience to become perfected in us? Don't give up. Just because you feel miserable doesn't mean that Jesus has given up on you.

Personal Life Coaching by Kim and Kathy

This workbook has introduced you to some new thinking, and understanding of the pain you are in. Some of you may desire personal mentoring/counseling/coaching through this difficult time in your life. After reading this book and our website, one of the best things you can do is sit and chat about your future.

Life-coaching is like having a personal pastor who will walk beside you on the road to Emmaus. We all need to hear words of life and encouragement from others who know how much we hurt and feel rejected. We all need to bounce our ideas and thoughts off some one else who lives in the Tree of Life.

If Kim or Kathy can serve you in this way, give us a call to discuss life-coaching. We are a servant ministry, so we charge a fraction of the fee for counseling that secular life-coaches charge. Our life-coaching involves a phone chat with Kim or Kathy once a week for one hour at a time. All conversations are totally confidential, and we keep no written records of this counseling. If you need love and encouragement to help you move and grow in the Tree of Life, give us a call and find out more. God bless you with healing! 918-542-2141.